FINDING MY WAY

Memories of a Czech Dissident,

1939 – 2008

by

Tomas Bisek

English Translation by Daniela and Tomas Bisek

British Library Cataloguing in Publication Data:
a catalogue record for this publication
is available from the British Library

ISBN   978-1-871828-89-4

Typeset in 11pt Minion Pro at Haddington, Scotland

Printing and cover design by
West Port Print and Design, St Andrews

Published with assistance from
the Drummond Trust,
3 Pitt Terrace, Stirling

This thrilling book is a brave personal account of life in the dark period of Czechoslovak history in the 1970s and 80s, and of a new life and new reality discovered in exile in Scotland. It will move the reader to feel with the minister and his family in their personal struggles, their doubts and their joys. Their story illuminates the universal realities of oppression, resistance and exile which recur throughout human history.

Magdalena Trgalova, Minister of the Evangelical Church of Czech Brethren; Minister of the Church of Scotland in Stromness, 2013 to 2015

Tomas Bisek's book reads like a novel: a young man graduates in engineering, studies to become a Protestant minister, and is welcomed in a country village parish. However his upholding of truth and human rights offends the communist regime and he is continually interrogated, barred from the pulpit and sent to work in the hills as a wood-cutter. Eventually he is forced to leave the country. In exile in Scotland, he serves as Presbyterian minister until after the Velvet Revolution when the family is allowed to return home. This unique life story illustrates the problems faced by Christians under Soviet occupation.

Prof. Petr Pokorny, D.D., D.Sc., D.Hon. New Testament Studies, the Protestant Theological Faculty, Charles University, Prague

This book is an exciting, retrospective examination of the author's remarkable and often perilous journey. His depiction brings to life the drastic changes of jobs, homes and circumstances that he and his family endured under the pre-1989 Communist regime in Czechoslovakia. Serious as it is in its exposure of human hypocrisy and betrayal in words and deeds, it is also written with humour and grace. The deep, sometimes agonizing but essentially uplifting questions the author constantly addresses to himself are raised also for the reader. Though the story was written primarily for those who lived through it in the former Czechoslovakia, it will be appreciated by all who are aware of the fragile nature of the accommodations we all make in our search for truth and for a spiritual home on this earth.

Petr Macek, Th.D., Ph.D., Systematic Theology, the Protestant Theological Faculty, Charles University, Prague

Tomas Bisek 'finds his way' with humility, courage and determination on a life's journey littered with obstacles which would defeat a person of lesser faith. In this moving memoir, he writes of his battle with the Communist authorities in former Czechoslovakia in a way which reminds me of Bonhoeffer's struggle against the totalitarianism of Nazi Germany; and the story of his journey into exile in Scotland, with his young family, in the 1980's, seems to speak directly to the experiences, good and bad, of today's migrants and asylum seekers. A book to lift your heart, and strengthen your faith. What a story!

John Harvey, former Leader of the Iona Community

This book is written with understatement – itself a product of living under a regime which forbade free speech. Yet here is the pedigree of dissent. The author describes the silence of his parents on political matters, recognising that they were heirs of a centuries-long tradition of dissent in Czech history.

Tracing the development of Bisek's own independence of thought, we are led through the menace and terror of secret surveillance and repression to the day when the pastor and his wife decide to flee with their four children to Scotland.

Even in a country so different from his own, Bisek finds that the church provides a continuity of work, life, identity and hope. Then the end of the Cold War enables him to return home. This fascinating book is a story to cherish.

John Miller, Moderator of the General Assembly of the Church of Scotland 2001-02

Speaking truth to power can have serious consequences, as Tomas and Daniela Bisek found in Communist Czechoslovakia.

This understated, yet chilling, account by an outspoken minister of the Gospel, and signatory to Charter 77 – whose manse was bugged by the Orwellian secret services – is a 'must-read'.

Ron Ferguson, Journalist and Minister at large

Contents

We grope for the wall like the blind, we grope like those who have no eyes . . . we look for justice, but there is none; for salvation, but it is far from us.

Isaiah 59:10-11 (RSV Bible)

Lord, spread wide the hem of your garment . . .

(In response to Mark 5:25-34)

For our grandchildren

For our Scottish friends

Acknowledgements

Very many people have helped to produce this book.

My thanks go first to those who, though separated from us by the Iron Curtain (1985-89), supported us through the initial five years of our exile in Scotland. Their reactions to my letters home encouraged me to continue writing them and, later, use them for the middle part of the book (Chapters 14 – 18). Those who shared our struggles prior to our leaving for Scotland are named in Chapter 9. There are, however, others who stimulated my thinking and my writing. One of them was the Moderator of the Evangelical Church of Czech Brethren, Milan Hajek, who had vigorously opposed our engagement in Charter 77. And yet, when he had read some of my letters from our exile in Scotland, he began writing to me in spite of knowing that the State Security most probably monitored his letters.

Shortly after I had retired, I worked as a volunteer for the Iona Community on the Island of Iona, where I was diagnosed with aggressive but curable lymphoma, which needed immediate treatment in Scotland. With deep gratitude I will always remember especially the empathic approach of the staff at Gartnavel Hospital and at the Beatson Cancer Centre in Glasgow. My wife, Daniela, and I spent a great part of the year in Glasgow in three different homes offered by loving friends: Sally Beaumont, Mary and John Miller, and Molly and John Harvey. These I name with my particular thanks for their generous provision of space for me to convalesce and to write.

At that time Alastair Hulbert stepped in and offered to go over Daniela's translation of my writing. We agreed that the text should not lose its 'CzEnglish veneer'. We are grateful to him for the encouragement he constantly kept giving us, and the many hours he spent over the text.

With sincere thanks I remember John Harvey's pertinent questions and suggestions.

Our son-in-law, Alan Miller, is to be thanked for explaining and correcting some words and passages, thanks to his acquaintance with the Czech language and circumstances.

In 2012 my book was published in Czech with the title *Ohledávání, doma, ve Skotsku a zase doma* by the Kalich publisher Michal Plzak in the Czech Republic.

The English version of the book had to wait till Mary and John Miller quite unexpectedly suggested going through the text once again. With new energy and stimulated especially by Mary, we found ourselves in the full swing of exchanges negotiating the meanings of particular words, passages, idioms, the setting of chapters and the flow of events with her very careful regard to the message of the book and its potential reader. Therefore our deepest gratitude goes to Mary for all her sensitive support and many hours of diligent work.

I also thank John for his reading the script several times, his never-ending encouragement and his constant belief that the book should be published in English.

I would like also to name my brother Petr. His expertise as a printer led him to spot details hidden from us. I thank him for his help.

My thanks also go to Jock Stein and Handsel Press for bringing *Finding My Way* to readers in English, and to the Drummond Trust for their support.

Finally, I must express my deep thanks to Daniela, who has been part of fifty years of my life and so we shared together the events described in the book. We have both frequently sensed the presence of the ultimate Actor in our ups and downs. May he spread his garment wide over us and bring his healing and peace to all.

Chapter 1

CHILDHOOD

I have gone over my beginnings several times in my mind. Rather than seeing the facts as I understood them in my early adulthood, I now seem to be closer to remembering what happened as one remembers a dream. So I am going to begin to delve into my own life and I wonder what meaning will emerge.

I was born at the beginning of World War II. Its end, after five years, marks the beginning of my search. I can hear my father say after he came home from the barricades in Prague, "When all this finishes, the self-styled 'heroes' will emerge." I wonder whether I understood what he meant. Throughout my life I have asked myself, 'What is true heroism?'

In a further memory I see the Emmaus Monastery on fire, from the terrace of our house on Dobeska Hill. The allies had arrived . . . The image of that fire later blended with my memory of fireworks at celebrations. I used to look out from our terrace over the River Vltava towards the Petrin Hill and watch the celebrations for Labour Day and the end of World War II, at the time of the so-called 'development of socialism and communism'. This 'development' didn't get in the way of the appreciation of the fireworks for a curious boy. But socialism and communism were not spoken about at home. It was as if their development gave my family no cause for celebration.

Now school begins. For children in the first year of school the teacher is like a second mother. She bestows praise and kisses. When we go off for three weeks on a school trip to the mountains, she looks after everything, even organizes a dance for the boys and girls. It seems like a dream; will this heady feeling last for long?

We got rolls, milk and yoghurt at school, but it was futile to try to make children take cod liver oil. I was the only one to take a swig from the bottle on the way home from school. I can still see my friends' faces. I played the hero with my bottle of cod liver oil in the face of those who refused it. I was just showing off and I knew well what my favourite food was. It was well known in my family circle that green lentils and hard-boiled eggs or fried eggs were what I always wanted for my birthday dinner. And I still do.

The wooden school huts on Dobeska Hill, overlooking the old part of Branik, my part of the city, were surrounded by cherry trees. At the end of the school year, the good boys were allowed to pick cherries for the others. "Four in the basket, one in your mouth," insisted our teacher. A friend and I were sitting up in the tree counting: "One, two, three, four in the mouth, and one for the basket". Reliability, loyalty and a kind of integrity are likely to be displayed if they are publicly demanded. But they do not come naturally. Neither do they become naturally and permanently part of a person. The idea that there are good people and bad people, competent and incompetent people, is not realistic in everyday life. I don't know if I came to this conclusion just through growing up. I know that it has been a process and I learned from experience. The Bible maintains that "there is no-one good, not even one",[1] and that is a lasting principle.

At home, I wasn't aware of any of the political pressures of the time. The silence of my parents about events on the political scene acted as a natural, and to a great extent impenetrable, protective wall against the outer world. I would go out from home into a world which my parents did not interpret for us. However, my eyes sometimes told me what my ears did not. That happened at the funerals of President Edvard Benes and later of Jan Masaryk, Minister of Foreign Affairs. I can still see the long queues of people waiting to pay tribute to them; many in tears, anxious.

Thinking about it now, I am able to see the dangerous dilemma of my parents' generation: how much could they share with their children? They had had to cope with the cruel dismembering of an independent and democratic Czechoslovakia, established and led by the philosopher President Tomas Garrigue Masaryk just after the First

---

1 Mark 10:18, Romans 3:10-12, cf. Psalm 14:1-3, Micah 7:2.

World War when the Austrian Empire collapsed. Twenty years later the independent country was brutally divided. The Czech area was changed into the Protectorate of Bohemia, Moravia and Silesia under the terrorizing auspices of Nazi Germany; so President Edvard Benes, the successor and close friend of Masaryk, emigrated to Britain and led the Czechoslovak government from London. After the war the Czech and Slovak areas were reunited and Benes became President of the so called Second Czechoslovak Republic. However, three years later, the Czechoslovak Communist Party staged a coup d'état orchestrated by the Soviets under Stalin. That was the end of our parents' generation's 'dream of democracy'. The imposed authoritarian regime lasted until the Velvet Revolution in 1989.

I was just nine years old in 1948, and in my way I shared my parents' silence, because it gradually became dangerous to say a word of criticism outside the home.

Why didn't my parents welcome the communist takeover in the way many others did then? After all, the greater part of the country was freed from Hitler by the Red Army and then, after the Communists seized power, they mesmerized people by preaching a programme of utopian justice in which all citizens would share everything. How did my parents know enough to see through the devious ideological misuse of honeyed words by Stalin and others in power? They were amongst a few who remembered well Masaryk's thorough analysis in his two-volume work *Russia and Europe*, with his clear statement: "No, Russian Bolshevism is not for us."

I came from a middle class family. My mother, Lydie, was the daughter of a minister of the Reformed Church, Vlastimil Svatopluk Juren. My father, Frantisek, grew up in a Roman Catholic family and, like his father, was a civil engineer. He converted to the Protestant Evangelical Church of Czech Brethren under the influence of both the student organisation 'Academic YMCA' and of his fiancée's family. The Evangelical Church of Czech Brethren stemmed from the union of the Lutheran and the Reformed churches, the only non-Roman Catholic churches tolerated in the Austrian Empire since the battle on the White Mountain near Prague in 1620, when the Protestant side was defeated. Enforced Catholicization followed. The non-Catholic nobility and gentry were allowed to leave the country but the common people who persevered in staying non-Catholic suffered cruel persecution. It was only much later, when the Toleration Edict was issued in 1781, that 'Believers of the Lamb', that is the remnants of the non-Catholics, were allowed to establish their own congregations. However, not until the founding of Czechoslovakia 1918 could they have their own Church, the Evangelical Church of Czech Brethren. 'Evangelical' meaning 'according to the evangel, the Good News'; 'Czech', relating to the name of the nation; 'Brethren' because they called themselves the Unity of Brethren in the times of persecution.

Politically, my family were admirers of T. G. Masaryk and his clear and open vision of democracy within an alliance of friendly and independent European nations. Additionally, as Czech Brethren, my parents also became members of the Academic YMCA, the forum of young dedicated Christians who accepted neither Nazi nor Communist domination. It was only later during my military service as a conscript that I consciously adopted our family's Christian

tradition and the beliefs of the Czech Brethren as my own. Neither of these concerned me when I was a child.

My mother ruled our family together with her older sister, Marta, who lived with us. My father was quite tall in comparison to my mother and he was patient with the two domineering women. Going to church on Sunday was not open to discussion and it became a heavy burden for me when I was about ten years old. My energetic mother would not be convinced on Sundays that I was suffering from a fever and so should be allowed to stay at home instead of being made to run down the hill to the small wooden church at the foot of Branik Hill, whose rocky face rises above the River Vltava. To get over the frustration I felt at my fate, I would carve in the pew with my finger nails. When I was in the church many years later, I was rather sorry to find that the pews had been renovated and no longer bore any witness to my reluctance to suffer anything that did not involve a game of football, hide-and-seek or climbing the rocks behind the church.

We were growing up: out of the four children in our family, it was usually the two middle ones, Petr and I, who did things together. The oldest, Honza, never joined us. I don't see him playing football with us in the street. Neither do I see him playing ice-hockey on the frozen Vltava. Petr and I used to scoff at his girly way of ice skating. The two of us dreamt of skating with real 'Canadian' skates, the only proper ice-hockey ones. And then there was our youngest and the only girl, Doris – Dorinka. She arrived at the end of the war - too late to join our gang. We, the boys, certainly did not need her and neither did we want her. She was her daddy's girl. I remember when it was her turn to do the washing up, Petr and I would hiss, "How come that it's Dad washing up again instead of her?"

I don't remember Honza having any problems in his early years. Until high school, he was a hundred per cent prize winner. He was a son to be shown off to visitors. Sometimes we all had to stand together nicely, from the oldest to the youngest, and Mother presented us as a team of prize children. After leaving the local primary school, Honza went to a school in Vinohrady, in the centre of Prague and, rather unexpectedly, changed into a 'problem child' . . . our relationship is still painful.

My first summer camps were organized by local people. We spent a couple of weeks with children we knew from school or the neighbourhood. No-one took much care of us, although we had been taken out of our home surroundings. All kinds of activities were provided, but most of it was a waste of time. An older boy masturbated in front of much younger ones and there was bullying. My brother Petr was often the target. Soon he was taller than me and was constantly interfering in complicated situations; then he was beaten up. Sometimes, cautiously, I tried to stick up for him, so that at least there would be two of us facing the opposition. Once I talked Petr round and we escaped from the camp, where he was being bullied every day. We went over some hills to a village where our parents were holidaying. But there was no reprieve: they took us back. Bullying stopped, but mockery thrived.

I also went to a boys' church camp which was run on military lines. The leader introduced himself as Deacon Stanek. We, the three brothers, shared a room with our distant cousins from Vinohrady: Titus, Tomas and Vlada. Every night, just before lights-out, Deacon Stanek came in with a horrifying question, "So, how many for each of you?" It was time to deal with the 'sins' we had registered during the day. The victim, bent over the iron bedstead, first had to state how many sins there were and then he was given his ration of punishment on his bare bottom with a stick. Tomas and Vlada always had lots of sins in store. It was routine for them. I would put my fingers into my ears so as not to hear the strokes of the stick nor the whimpering and crying.

I got a proper beating once, when I didn't want to share some plum buns my mother had sent in a parcel. Sharing everything with everybody in the room was one of Stanek's principles. As I remember it, I saw in Deacon Stanek's actions the Evangelical Church shaping the whole world. However, a reluctance to give and to share has somehow stayed with me, although often concealed for the shame of it. I wonder therefore if I am living my life like the rich young man who turned sadly away from the most generous Giver.

Just before the Communist coup in Czechoslovakia in 1948, we were in a camp in Herlikovice in the Giant Mountains, where today there is a church holiday centre. The leaders, the three Soltesz brothers, provided two eventful weeks for us. One part of the programme was collective washing in a 'production line' in the open air. Every boy was first squirted with ice-cold water from a hose, then, at another station, he got soaped, next, he got sprayed all over and, finally, he was dried very roughly. Icy water, the reckless soaping of eyes, ears, buttocks, front, rubbing dry till the skin was red – all this was done by the three Solteszes briskly and vigorously. But the abundance of activities we enjoyed has stayed with me until now: excellent athletic competitions, a hike to the highest peak, Snezka *('Snow Peak'),* and back over the 'Kozi hrbety' *('Goat's Ridge'),* then still open to hikers.

Even now, when I am in the Giant Mountains, I look up at the hills with proud satisfaction that I once conquered them. I remember how I had to fight to be allowed to take part. Petr, although younger, was already bigger than me. He was taken to be 'Tomas', old enough to take part, and I, taken to be 'Petr', was too young and small to be allowed to go. Eventually, I won the battle for the truth and in the end, the real Petr was allowed to come too. Hurting deep in my soul, I made sure I walked at the front the whole day.

Around this time our GP sent me to a sanatorium in Harrachov, in the western part of the Krkonose Mountains, for three months, so that I could get 'fattened up'. Attempts to give us school lessons were elbowed out by almost daily skiing. And I experienced an excess of food. I was amazed that I could have a second and even a third sausage. We had hot cocoa on weekdays. The memory of a hefty St Bernard dog is my favourite one from Harrachov. He sometimes slept on the floor in the dining hall. Once he lay under our round table, where four of us were eating. The dog suddenly decided to leave. He got up and started to leave with our table balanced on his back!

Another thing I remember from Harrachov is a 'church' experience. A carer took us on her own initiative to Mass. She knelt and so did the other children. I was the only one who felt I couldn't. I felt ambivalent, and also ashamed that I was not able to kneel spontaneously in a way that expressed my solidarity with the others while yet remaining independent. The pressure of authority, and the strength of my desire to fit in with those around me, was very strong. I don't have this problem today. For example, I can kneel with Norwegian Lutherans, or in the Anglican Church in Garforth near Leeds, where our son Lukas lives. After a compelling biblical sermon on the Lord's Prayer, it is easy to kneel with others. But as a young boy, I experienced it as spiritual-ideological manipulation, in spite of a great deal of ignorance on my part, and I have never forgotten it. Today I am glad to experience liturgical practice that is connected with the proclamation of the Gospel, which is then conveyed by means of the liturgy. The Word thus becomes clearer and more convincing. It symbolizes the fact that the Good News we share is the Word which is to stay among us. It is the Word which has become flesh. It is not the other way round – that flesh became the Word. So these are the three snapshots from my stay in a sanatorium in Harrachov: Skiing, Mass and a St Bernard dog.

The memory of the St Bernard dog carrying the table leads me to memories of my encounters with animals at home. First, we had a dog, an Irish terrier. I remember a holiday where Siky was with us. He must have gained our respect, I sigh. There wasn't much fun with him. A long spell with cats followed. As a young school boy I learned that you can understand cats and relate to them not only by feeding them, but also because they need and like being near you and playing. I remember three Siamese cats: Bobesh, Caspar and Hashtal. All of them had short tails with a sort of hook at the end. They were grey and had black legs and black heads and ears.

Bobesh was a female and became an able mother. She always managed to find a drawer with our clothes in it for her kittens. No basket would confuse or attract her. Even when lifted by the tail, she would not stop purring. From my own experience I learned that a domestic animal is a living creature. I can have a relationship with it and expect a response, beyond what might be expected from an animal. Therefore, I suspect, it was relatively easy for me to accept living in a rural area. Animals there have a much greater significance – they have the role of being partners, not only for the pleasure of their company, but also for support, help, or as an instrument for work. At the same time, even a favourite animal can end up as food on the table; human beings demonstrate and preserve their dominant position.

After five years at junior school, I would run down the hill to the senior primary school in the 'Old School Building'. There were over thirty of us in the class. Discipline depended on the teachers, and we had to address them as 'Comrade'. I realize that I preferred not to address them at all; did the words we used at home influence me? But I don't remember that this was overt in my relationships with the teachers. My openness as a younger child and my willingness to please were over. I sat in the back row among my friends. I tried to extricate myself from the pressures of school. I wanted new experiences. We threw conkers over the wall from the school yard into the street when a teacher was coming. One of us, Standa, peed from an open window in the toilet straight onto the janitor's little daughter. Shortly afterwards, the janitor burst into the classroom. Ignoring the teacher, he shouted, 'Who's pissed on our little Mary's head?' The class roared with laughter. Nobody, as far as the teacher could discover.

A special chapter in my childhood was a number of summers when we, the whole family, stayed at Herlikovice again, this time at forest work camps. Trees were planted, grass was cut for upholstery, trees were felled and hay was made; these activities regularly took three weeks off our summer holidays. We stayed in small houses now known as the Mountain Home. We often walked to work up to Plan, about 5 km uphill. It was rather strenuous for Petr and me at first. I also remember how different families tackled the assigned tasks in various ways. I noticed how much, or how little, they exerted themselves; some appeared aloof from physical endeavour. Today, after having gained my own experience of hard work felling trees in the forest, I understand that physical exertion and endurance are not of a lower grade. They may sometimes cultivate determination to face a task, in spite of it (perhaps) being of a non-spiritual nature. It is unwise to make a distinction between the spiritual and physical realms. We do not live as spirits here on earth. We are made of flesh and bones.

Chapter 2

HIGH SCHOOL, GROWING UP AND MY FIRST JOB

Now I am in 'the eleven-year school' a new, socialist name for 'gymnasium', i.e. a grammar or high school. Our school was in a new building in Branik. It was just round the corner from the senior primary school.

TOMAS AND SIBLINGS

Eleven-year school was for me a period of intense friendships and encounters. I remember competitions in board games, chess and table tennis. We played football and in winter ice-hockey. There used to be the school cup skiing competition on the near-by slopes; the favourite run was called Cinglak. There were school skiing holidays in the mountains. A very dramatic skiing trip was to the Lucni mountain chalet in the Krkonose Mountains. We climbed the Lucni Mountain through the Blue Valley with rucksacks on our backs and skis on our shoulders. The temperature was well below zero and there was a blizzard. Darkness fell early. After dark, the Krkonose Mountain Rescue men joined us. I kept turning back and saw how some of my friends threw their skis in the snow and the members of the Rescue team encouraged them to continue with the climb. Some suffered frostbite of the ears or fingers. But we got there! The weather kept us at the Lucni chalet for two days. But then the sun shone and we skied in the fresh, powdery snow in the Blue Valley. Of course, there were no tows or lifts then. You could go down only after you had climbed up.

Our class existed under the rule of a resolute though highly-strung class teacher, Mrs Muzikova. She often dealt with issues unilaterally and according to her own understanding. Once she announced that we had all become, irrevocably, members of the Czechoslovak Union of Youth. In a similar way, students who were good at Czech had to work on getting the Fucik Award by reading (or not) prescribed and approved books. These were her idiosyncrasies.

Of course, I also remember serious problems, such as the class register being buried by three friends. We responded to a plea by a class beauty to get rid of an unfavourable entry in the register by making it disappear. All would have been well if one of us, it was Standa again, had not boasted about it. The rumour reached our class teacher and, consequently, we were given a low mark for conduct. I added to it a 'desertion' from military training. In my end of year school report I had ones and twos from some subjects and the lowest, three, for conduct.

As I look back, I realise that during my school years I never learned what it meant to study. School was for me an encounter with a system which deserved to be resisted. I wanted to be with my friends and there was also the beginning of eyeing-up girls. But in spite of all that, my final school report was good.

My school results, however, were not good enough for the Faculty of Nuclear Physics at the Czech Technical University in Prague and my disastrous performance in the entrance exams contributed to my being an unsuccessful applicant. I had better luck at the Faculty of Economics with Engineering, from which however, I graduated as a mechanical engineer, because in the third year my specialisation was changed to Engineering with Economics. I spent the five years of studies suppressing my yearning for freedom, something I became fully aware of only after I graduated and started my first job. I realised that I could, ultimately, make decisions about my own life.

I regarded my studies as an unavoidable annoyance. My heart started turning in a different direction. It originated in my encounters at church work camps. We, the three Bisek brothers, started to take part in them at the same time. Honza belonged with the older ones, but Petr and I were always together. I see a picture from a work camp in the Jizerske Mountains, west of the Krkonose Mountains: instead of working, we sit around. The leader, Blaza Sourek, appears from nowhere and says, "So you call this work?" We go back to work in the forest very ashamed. But I liked the hard work. As a young boy, at a work camp with my parents, I enjoyed cutting grass for upholstery. I saw my father cut down trees with other 'amateurs', mainly townspeople. In my romantic dreams I saw myself working in the forest one day.

Working in the forests and meadows of the Jizerske and the Jeseniky mountains, in the north of Moravia, gradually stopped being the most important thing for me. It was the fellowship of young people that became significant. Was I looking in two directions at the same time? I knew I had to concentrate on my studies; in my heart, though, I was devoted to the young people from the camps.

There were a great number of these summer work camps. Everything was done on the basis of voluntary work and there was no institutional backing. I am still amazed at how people at these camps spontaneously met and both accepted old friends and made new ones. I became so committed that I even accepted the responsibility of leadership of some of them.

In my memory I see us all sitting and talking around a camp fire at our log cabin. Suddenly a figure, someone we didn't know, came out of the darkness and said:

"Good evening. Who is the Chief? I'm Sheriff."

I said, "But we're not guilty. We haven't done anything."

The newcomer explained, "It's my name and I need to see the Chief to introduce myself."

I still don't understand why as a Chief I didn't start wearing a lovely Red Indian head dress and carrying a bow and arrows.

How natural it seemed to us that all this would go on year after year. We could not see any possibility that these camps might stop. Our only worry was to get them organised. Negotiations with the local forestry commission were rather straightforward; we had to go and see them early in spring and negotiate the conditions. During the summer holidays several two-week-long camps took place. Each of them was attended by up to thirty or forty young people. We worked about eight hours a day in the forest or meadows. I remember the morning and evening informal worship. We played lots of games. We went on long walks at weekends and, of course, we held never-ending discussions. Without these summer camps I would not have got to know so many friends. I still meet some of them. And without these summer camps, it would not have been possible for me, a man from Prague, to spend my life with Daniela, a woman from Sumperk, a town in northern Moravia.

The spirit of the camps was one of deep understanding and joy. I do not remember another instance of a need for moral encouragement or reproof for not working diligently enough after that first one, directed at my brother and me, in the Jizerske mountains. At these camps we

tried together to understand what the Bible said; we were interested in how the person leading us in the short worship understood it and we also tried to make out the meaning of the songs we sang, the discussions we had and the prayers we shared. Our communal life took place in a very basic hut or an old cottage, where we shared cooking and housework, going out to work, discussions, playing games and getting to know one another – all that created a framework full of joy, trust and understanding. The beautiful, then still unspoiled, countryside was an integral part of it all. We earned almost nothing and never questioned it. I remember especially one summer when there was a competition on: which camp will spend the least on food? We did not starve. We did not need much more than porridge oats, sardines, bread and a few more essentials. Fruits of the forest enhanced our menu: wild strawberries, raspberries, blueberries or mushrooms. I remember most vividly dumplings filled with blueberries.

It was in these camps that the first encounters took place: boys met girls. These 'couples' would stay up until the early hours. The leaders in charge tried to discover and check up on them. I remember Reverend Cihak and his torch. He would shine it into the darkness to see if there was a couple trying to disappear from the circle round the camp fire. A friend of mine, Jan Dittrich, and I were a pair of unrestrained pranksters who found pleasure in teasing the leader. Once, walking away from the fire, we put our arms round each other's waists. The torch spotted us immediately. We went back with a loud guffaw.

A couple of years later, I was well aware of the girls who were around. This time we were on a skiing holiday and stayed in one of the huts. I fell deeply in love. I tried to draw Verka's attention either by showing off my skiing skills, which was easy thanks to my Harrachov experience, or by playing my recorder, which I always carried with me.

Now I know that to attract someone you do not have to show off to look better, especially by attempting something a little beyond your abilities. On the other hand, certain qualities, skills and boldness work to your advantage. For some of us the time spent with one another in endless talk turned into love. I experienced this with Verka on that skiing holiday. Our relationship grew stronger through writing letters, but we met only occasionally; a boy from Prague and a girl from Brno.

I would like to mention very briefly the gradual beginnings of a particular friendship between Karel Trusina, Jan Dittrich and myself. This manifested itself in a distinct, intuitive affinity – a mutual attraction through words, looks and feelings. We made up a place name, 'Yoorashov'. For several years, it was a magic word over which we made a lot of fuss: to call 'Yoorashov' into a dark corner or gutter, or to say 'Yoorashov' when a complication arose was an act that had a definite meaning for us. Jan and I discovered how playful and joyful Karel was and, at the same time, how he worked extremely hard, sometimes, when necessary, without stopping. I saw him accepting and passing on the Good News in the course of the day in a very secular manner, accessible and down-to-earth. He made it clear for me that it is living faith, rather than talking about it, that matters. Talking should happen rather less often and in a quiet voice. Karel also helped me to see how it can be counter-productive to use the name of Jesus Christ and God too often and in vain; then it is close to a swear word.

The beginning of my working life happened as expected. After graduation as an engineer I had a placement in TOS – a machine tool factory in Holoubkov near Pilsen. I started in an office where I dealt with numbers and figures. I saw no sense in it. After all my schooling and studies, was I supposed to sit in an office not knowing anything about the manufacturing processes? What did all the figures and indices mean? I protested. Following the example of Tomas Bata, the entrepreneur and founder of the shoemaking company of the same name, I requested that I be allowed to spend the first year going round all the departments on the shop floor. Only then would I be able to see how the factory worked, what the figures meant and what I should do with them.

All was agreed and authorised by the directors. My first post was at a 'drawing board' where crude casts were marked with the principle dimensions, from which other measurements were taken, so that the cast could be cut to shape, pared, drilled, etc. It was as if you put a virtually finished product on a cast, so that it could be worked from all sides. I was quite quick and finished the work soon. I went to the shop floor manager to get something more to do. After some time, it became harder and harder to find him; I must have been annoying him. I was bored at first but then I would sit at the drawing board with an English vocabulary book in my hand. He could not ignore this. He approached me and asked me not to undermine the morale of the other employees. After that I would go to the changing room and read.

As the first year was drawing to an end, I went through a strange inner transformation and asked myself a basic question: what next? The directors were unable to keep their word and make it possible for me to get experience in all the departments. This contributed to my uncertainty and I felt that I would not return to the factory after military service.

I sensed that my orientation in life was changing in a radical way. During my studies at the Technical University and the employment that followed, I was gradually moving in a very different direction – towards the vocation of a minister of religion. My interest in the meaning of the Biblical message had grown under the influence of the fellowship of the work camps and also the Bible study courses organised by the Church. There I met Revd Karel Trusina, who was responsible for youth work. He had a great influence on me and I grew into seeing the Good News as authentic. I started to feel closer to the Bible; my reverence for it became permanent.

Chapter 3

MILITARY SERVICE – MOVING TO THEOLOGY

It was military service that brought the turning point in my life. I served in Podborany, a small town north-west of Prague, with a tank regiment. Graduates from the Technical University were normally posted as squad commanders. I was the only one who was not ranked in a similar way, as if I did not fit into the system. There was a vacancy for the post of regimental technical engineer, because the electrical engineering officer had gone to an English course, and so I became a temporary lieutenant in the technical department. I supervised electrical equipment in the repair station of the regiment. I was in charge of the army electricians responsible for the tank batteries and the personnel working there. In addition, I trained officers, so that they could understand the principle of tank stabilizers. For me it meant reading the relevant military texts which were written in clear language. It was not difficult to understand why the gun did not change its position when the tank went up and down in the terrain. There were gyroscopes which transferred the angle of movement to the hydraulic system which, in turn, tilted the gun against the movement of the tank in a fraction of a second and kept the gun in the same aiming position. I was admired by the officers for how I understood it. I, on the other hand, noticed their inability – or rather their reprehensible laziness – to read such a simple text.

During the year I became acquainted with the combat (in)efficiency of the armies of the Warsaw Pact. There were several field exercises which I always spent next to the regimental technician engineer, Novotny, in his armoured personnel carrier. During the preparations, the alert and the departure for a night field exercise, I felt that Jaroslav Hasek's Josef Svejk (from *Good Soldier Svejk*) was always nearby. For example, several days' notice was always given before the next field exercise and the tank drivers had plenty of time to get ready. At the time of departure, however, there were usually several tanks that could not get started because their batteries were still being recharged. I still don't understand it; and I don't understand why it somehow always got overlooked.

Being placed at the regimental office offered fantastic advantages. I was registered and accommodated with a unit of soldiers, but I was not one of them. Due to my daily presence in the office I was separated from the life of the regiment. On the other hand, I was similarly separated from the life of the office because I had all my meals with the soldiers. Being in two places at the same time sometimes enabled me to disappear. Once I nearly got into trouble when I left for Prague and a regimental field exercise was organised the next day, which meant that no one was supposed to be in the barracks. On my return, having broken a seal on the door and 'replaced' it with something I found, I hid in the dormitory until the following morning. I hoped that the staff-sergeant would not have time to examine the seal to see whether it corresponded with his stamp. He didn't.

Not having a normal rank meant that I did not get the pay that graduates from the Technical University usually received. I soon discovered that the regimental clerk was also a graduate and we built up a sort of friendship. After some time, I asked him if he would show me my file, which was top secret, so that I could see why I was not treated like other graduates. He bluntly refused, saying that he did not want to end up in prison. However, a few days later, he told me what was in my file: "Not to be ranked, for State Security reasons regarding his father."

His trust astonished me. Several months later, a military prosecutor came to inspect our regiment. I requested a hearing. When he invited me in, I asked him to examine the reason why I had not been given a rank. I argued that it was not possible to say that there were "State Security reasons regarding my father" without a proper explanation. That was a very dangerous thing to say. He promised he would look into it and asked me to come again at the end of his inspection, which I did. He told me that there were no political reasons and that it was only a matter of numbers. I knew he was lying. He knew he was lying too but he had no idea that I knew. There was nothing else I could do except say, "Thank you for your explanation". After some days, I told my friendly clerk about it. He gave me a laconic reply: "Next time I'll show nothing to no-one".

The rest of my year in the army is hard to describe because of what I experienced. I had plenty of time to read the Bible. The booklet *For Every Day* by Professor Adolf Novotny (Bible texts with short meditations) was for me a very good resource and help. It led me through the darkness of military life, of which there was too much every day. It got into my ears – my weak point. I suffered from an inflammation of the Eustachian tube for several weeks; and my hearing was terribly impaired. I do not think that military service hardens the body and character. Just the opposite! It is often a damaging experience for those who are not anchored in their families or friendships. During my own time in the military I was given sustenance also by Professor Novotny's wonderfully understandable words.

The end of my relationship with Verka came during my year as an army conscript. I was a dejected soldier and she had just started her studies in Prague. The loneliness of a soldier boosted my yearnings. On the other hand, my love for Verka was affected by my unhappy army experiences. When we met, instead of expressing my joy at being with her, I tended to lament the incidents in the army. The worst was what was happening to the new recruits, called 'pheasants' in Czech slang. The old hands would bully and torment many of them; sometimes they chose brutal and sordid methods. I knew that some of the recruits were in danger of even taking their own lives, while I was snug in the regimental office with no authority to interfere. As I unloaded all this on to Verka, our relationship became strained.

After the break-up, Verka met Daniela at a work camp and told her everything about this fellow who had "changed so unbelievably from a fantastic and happy chap into somebody who just whinged all the time . . . and that's it". How then Daniela fixed her eyes on me and even decided to stay at my side for ever is a very pleasant mystery.

While I was still in the army, the influence of work camps, courses and other gatherings, as well as reading and searching for what to do next, led me to make a decision: I would try to take advantage of the low number of applicants for the Comenius Theological Faculty. What if I applied? Perhaps part time study would be permitted? I needed a reference from my employer in my application. Because I was a soldier that meant getting a reference from my military superior. In my case it was the technical engineer of the regiment, Major Novotny, a graduate from the Military Technical Academy in Moscow. "I have to try to ask him", I said to myself. I had nothing to lose. Very often I felt that I was far too hesitant, but this time I did not see any other way.

Moreover, I did not think I should give up without attempting it first. I never had any conflicts with Major Novotny, as he was a courteous man. Sometimes he even showed his satisfaction at how I fulfilled his orders. I remember that on this occasion I approached his office hesitantly and hoped that he would come out. He did not and so I had to knock and open the door myself:

"Corporal Bisek. May I have permission to speak, sir?"

"Right," he replied. "What can I do for you?"

"I need to speak to you," I said.

"I'm listening," he said.

I started to explain, "Comrade Major, I need a reference from you for an application to study at university."

He replied, "But you have finished your degree, haven't you?" and continued, "What is it that you need? I'm satisfied with you. Show it to me. I'll sign it. "

"Comrade Major, it is for a first degree," I said.

"So, another one? What is it going to be?" he asked.

"Theology," I replied.

There was a long pause. Then Major Novotny said, "Sit down." He was quiet and kept looking at me. Then he said, "Nonsense." There was another pause and he said, "I'm a Roman Catholic but I can't tell anybody. There's no future in it. Why do you want to do it?" There was another long pause. Then he continued in a down to earth way, "Look, I'm thoroughly satisfied with you. If I ask you to do something, I can forget about it. I have no reason not to give you a good reference. You know what? I'll say that I recommend that you study at university. I won't mention theology. I'm sorry I can't do anything more for you."

I replied after a pause, "I sincerely thank you, Comrade Major. I couldn't have asked for anything more from you."

Novotny remarked, "I don't know why you want to study theology, but it's your business. I hope you won't be disappointed. Good luck."

He shook hands with me in a non-soldierly way. I left feeling moved.

We never returned to that subject again, although I had a feeling that we now had something in common. It was one of those experiences that brought home to me that it can be deceptive to judge people according to first impressions. If possible, it is only proper to approach others without preconceptions but with positive expectations.

I applied for the Faculty of Theology with determination and subsequently received an invitation for an interview. I asked for leave and went to Prague in my uniform. It was so strange that I began to accept it all as something that might be normal.

I think I have a piece of advice that can be helpful in interview situations: do not succumb to your emotions, excitement or the feeling of being special. React as naturally as you can, simply and, if possible, directly; otherwise you will be isolated and fail to connect with others, because they do not perceive the situation as you do. I remember how once in later life, at a meeting of the Europe Committee of the Church of Scotland, I listened to Dr Nansie Blackie describing the atmosphere of an ecumenical gathering in Basel in a very excited way, hoping that she could arouse in us the same feeling of excitement so that we would get carried away by it. It did not work. I remarked that we had not had her experience; we had not been there. This is no doubt also valid about the work camps I describe so warmly – so, do you feel any special excitement when I reminisce?

I remember only the final part of my interview at the Theological Faculty. The chairman, the Vice Dean of the Faculty, Professor Josef Soucek, asked me about the reference I had received from the army. He said, "Brother Bisek, we have known your evangelical family for many years, also from the times of the Academic YMCA.[1] Therefore there is no need for us to ponder whether you realise what you are letting yourself in for. But how are you going to explain to the committee that you have a recommendation from the army? It has never happened before."

My recounting of the conversation with Major Novotny caused general amusement. In the end, Professor Soucek confirmed the Faculty's interest in accepting me. He added, however, that it would not be possible without an intervention by the Dean of the Faculty, Professor Josef Lukl Hromadka, at the Ministry of Culture, which did not surprise me. I was glad and I returned to my army unit in Podborany in a happy frame of mind.

It was astonishing that the Ministry complied with Professor Hromadka's request and I was allowed to study for a second degree. The condition was, however, that I would have to study full-time for

1 The Academic YMCA was banned after 1948.

five years, not part time, so that a precedent would not be set for the future, and studying for more degrees would not be encouraged. I did not feel an urge to understand the logic. Moreover, a vision of becoming an eternal student was quite pleasing to me although it was something I had not reckoned with. And so, in October 1964 I moved to the Seminary in V Jircharich Street and started attending lectures and seminars. A completely new and unexpected chapter in my life began.

Chapter 4

A STUDENT OF THEOLOGY

It was clear right from the beginning that the life of a student of theology at the Comenius Faculty in Prague had two basic parts: in the Seminary and at the Faculty. I still see it as a great privilege that even students whose homes were in Prague could live together in the Seminary. This was possible because the number of students was kept very low by the authorities and there was room for everybody who was accepted to study. Early morning translation from the biblical languages, followed by a short period of worship before breakfast, was a routine that many of us remember fondly now. Discussions and various activities were another important aspect of our life in the Seminary.

We were one big family of students. This experience showed me how important it is to supplement individual study with communal activity which complements education and makes it more down to earth. I matured very gradually to the state that is called 'conversion'. I was invariably encouraged by the combination of fellowship on the one hand and withdrawal and searching on the other. Both are essential for me.

The time of the middle sixties did not let us remain in seclusion, away from the outside world. Its existence was made real for us in the cartoon-like figure of Professor Polak. He was appointed by the Ministry of Culture to teach us so-called social science. We derided his expositions of an ideal social order for which our society was heading. He made it easy for us to mock him because he frequently told us how we, students of theology, and churches would disappear into the black hole of history.

Everybody, of course, had to sit Polak's exams: the theory of Marxism-Leninism, scientific Communism and the history of the workers' movement. These were compulsory subjects at all universities. I did not think Professor Polak was dangerous. His motives seemed to me easily understood, and very boring. Was he perhaps concealing that he had also been commissioned as an informer? The fact that he was a member of the Faculty Council and was always present meant that it was difficult to discuss sensitive things and it also hindered open conversation.

Let me touch briefly on what our teachers at the Faculty endowed us with. When I was a student, the director of the Seminary, Professor Jan Milic Lochman, lived there too with his family. Without his constant effort to keep a strict regime we would not have managed to get together very early in the morning to practise translations from the biblical languages and have a short period of worship which we prepared ourselves. It was not easy to address one's fellow students who made up a very critical forum. The range of the students' attitudes was very varied and it was not easy to find those who you were spiritually related to.

Professor Jan Milic Lochman introduced us in an excellent way to ancient Greek philosophy, as well as to modern philosophy. He also taught systematics. I remember regular skiing holidays with him in the Krkonose Mountains. Professor Lochman reigned on the snow unchallenged and it bothered us. We conceived a naughty idea to show him that he could not always be first: several of the fastest skiers started skiing downhill making it look obvious that they would be the fastest down the slope. That was an invitation for the professor. He skilfully overtook one after another and we soon saw him in front of everybody. Further down, however, a skier appeared from nowhere, as if by magic, and was the first to arrive. As the rest of us got there, we saw Professor Lochman shaking his head. He said, "How is it possible, brother, that I didn't see you? I would certainly have gone faster. I don't understand it. Congratulations." We secretly sniggered at this undeclared competition and we did not divulge anything. However, Lochman returned to the subject at dinner. He wondered aloud how it could have happened. We could not hold it in any longer and confessed that the 'winner' had hidden in the forest and joined the 'race' at the right time. We all laughed. Oh no! Brother Professor did not laugh. Instead, he gave us a lecture about fair play: the honour of sportsmen, let alone students of theology, does not allow them to cheat in such a way! His mood became very grim. He would not speak to us. We left the table in disgrace.

He did not speak to us the next morning. He went skiing before anybody else and skied on his own the whole day. Our attempts to apologise did not ease the situation. The whole trip remained marked by the incident.

Of course, I also remember his ability and readiness to translate from and into the world languages. His accuracy of expression and thought was remarkable; so was the high standard of his preparation and exposition. It certainly was not an accident that he was later elected Chancellor of the University of Basel, Switzerland, for two consecutive terms.

Professor Lochman and I met again in Scotland after nearly thirty years. He was one of the speakers at a Summer School in St Andrews. His excellent lectures were on the Czech Reformation. He spoke about Jan Hus, Petr Chelcicky, Jan Amos Komensky (Comenius), and others. It was there that I heard how Komensky had to walk from Heidelberg in Germany to his village in Moravia with a load of books on his shoulders, because he had spent all his money on books!

I also remember how Jan Milic took me by the elbow and said: "Brother Bisek, let's go and find the place where the Hussite martyr, Pavel Kravar (Paul Crawar), was burned at the stake on 23rd July 1433." And he went on, "When I studied here just after the Second World War, I found a cross in the pavement."

Memories of my years of study of theology take me to two other professors: Amedeo Molnar and Josef B. Soucek. My esteem for them endures. Professor Molnar instilled in me that it is imperative to be aware of history in everyday life, because otherwise we will live our lives as individuals or communities marooned in time. He kept introducing us to ancient witnesses of the faith. Professor Molnar put before us the Waldensians, both Calvinist and Lutheran Reformations, the Czech Brethren – all these and lots more. He encouraged us to use the National Library and gave us practical advice. He also taught us rhetoric; his usage of Czech was outstanding. It was clear that he was realistic in seeing that most of his students did not have the thorough preparation of a grammar school education.

Professor Soucek, a New Testament scholar who had studied in Aberdeen for a year, was very much appreciated because of his way of using contemporary examples, thus fixing the biblical message in the present, in our minds, our culture and civilisation, as well as in the changing world. His exposition made it clear to me that the Good News about the living Christ can be taken as a creed which, although perhaps distant, is not alien to the discerning mind that compares how things were then with how they are now. His analyses of the New Testament were always interwoven with Old Testament texts which carried a clear message as the basis for the New Testament. It was not a forced unity; God's unique concern for his people was manifested then in his accompanying them, and was fully accomplished in Jesus of Nazareth. Soucek also explained to us Paul's missionary ardour, through clear reasoning and sensitive witness. I found the exposition of the drama of Easter in his booklet, *The Suffering of the Lord according to the Gospels*, excellent. I read it in one go when I had a nasty bout of 'flu and I keep returning to it.

Professor Rudolf Rican gained my special admiration. He taught history. I found his lectures difficult because I was not patient and disciplined enough to listen to his monotonous voice and the gradual development of his arguments. On the other hand, I saw him fully involved in the deliberations of the Faculty Council, where I used to sit as the students' representative. He did not tolerate injustice. It greatly embarrassed him when his colleagues were too assertive. With no hesitation he pressed hard that the doctoral candidates who had not been able to graduate for political reasons some years before should be awarded their degrees. I remember how he asked me once what I intended to do after graduating and I responded in a rather romantic way that I would like to use both my qualifications as a missionary somewhere in the developing world. He did not let my response rest without remarking, "Brother Bisek, I think there is a need for mission here, at home."

He was right. He could not have known, however, that the totalitarian powers would blow us across the Channel to Scotland for several years. Such a 'mission' could not have occurred to anyone. Professor Rican had spent a year in the twenties as a student of theology in Glasgow – the city where I worked in the nineties. It was he who was with me and Daniela at the beginning of our life together. Having blessed our marriage at a service in the Church of St Martin's in the Wall, he regularly visited us in our small room in the Seminary and brought the best butter or a jar of Ovaltine; as if he was the forerunner of the dear folk in the village of Teleci, my future charge, who were extremely generous and would bring eggs and meat to the manse.

One of the special features of the Seminary was that students from the Hungarian Reformed Church in Slovakia had to study at

Our Wedding Day

the Theological Faculty in Prague. The Czechoslovak government did not allow them to study just over the Hungarian border, where they would have been in their own tradition, language and near their homes. That was the extent of the brotherhood of nations in one political block! The Warsaw Pact did not allow free traffic between the member countries. For example, visitors from the USSR would always be required to stay in a tight group that was led and controlled by guides.

Hungarian applicants, often from distant small villages in the most eastern part of Slovakia, had to go through the same interview as anyone else. However, the interviewing committee had to make allowances for their mother tongue and the extent to which they knew what the theology course would be about. As the students' representative, I was invited to be present at these interviews. I remember a Hungarian applicant who was not able to answer a single question. In despair, the secretary of the Faculty said, "Brother Bela, tell us, who was Jesus Christ?" Brother Bela thought very hard and then said in the Slovak language, "It's difficult to say who Christ was". He was accepted after this successful answer.

Today I know how some of them, including a professor at the Theological Faculty in Komarno in Slovakia, remember their studies in Prague with gratitude. Some of them still read the works of our translators of the Bible; they gratefully keep in touch with the Prague Faculty and their former fellow students.

I did have a problem, however, with a certain member of the teaching staff. I falter as I try to describe the course of my encounters with Professor Milan Opocensky. Am I trying to recall something that I could or should have left behind by now? Can I resolve it now? Use your own judgement.

The trip of the first Russian astronaut, Yuri Gagarin, into space was seen as a great achievement. We learned that he had not met God in space. There was a photograph of space, as Gagarin captured it, displayed on a big board in the Seminary. The caption said: "Historic Event". It only needed a black pen and the historic event became a "Hysterical Event". A mischievous resident of the Seminary, where a lot of pranks were played almost daily, had not reckoned that there would be somebody who would feel obliged immediately and in orthodox fashion to defend the Party and the Government. It was brother Opocensky, who also resided in the Seminary and who voiced his deep concern: he declared that what had happened on the display board was "a desecration of a great moment in the history of mankind. The culprit must bear the most serious consequences". I lived in fear and uncertainty expecting an action which would mean the end of my studies – but nobody informed on me.

Another encounter with Professor Opocensky was at his instigation. He approached me and said that he had spoken to a clerk at the Ministry of Culture and suggested that I be a delegate to a World Student Christian Federation (WSCF) conference in Geneva. I thought that the students should elect their representative, but he did not agree and added that he had already had to name somebody and I was the students' representative anyway.

I hastened to speak with Professor Rican, one of my favourite teachers. He was a historian, and I asked him what I should do. "Forgive him. It's his way of doing things. It's not right, but you're the students' representative. It will be good if somebody goes." He tried to calm me down.

Time went by. Professor Opocensky was abroad and I was waiting impatiently for what would happen. Not long before the conference I bumped into him in the street; it was rather unexpected. I felt awkward but asked nevertheless what was happening regarding the conference. "Didn't I tell you?" Professor Opocensky replied and continued, "The Ministry had, unfortunately, some objections. So, perhaps, another time . . ."

I was to meet Professor Opocensky again at various stages in my later life, and the relationship was never to be easy.

My years at theological college did not consist only of studying. Again, there were work camps, to which other youth group activities were gradually added, such as rambling and going rowing or canoeing on a river. I remember our walking in the Belanske Tatry, a mountain range east of the High Tatras in Slovakia. We stayed in hay-lofts which we rated as 'one-mouse', 'two-mouse' or 'three-mouse' lodgings. Daniela's pen-pal from East Germany, Birgit, was with us. She was not used to our way of spending holidays and was surprised at our being happy to carry all we had on our backs. Daniela tried to make it easier for her; I see a picture of Birgit, tall and robust, with a tiny rucksack and next to her Daniela, who was shorter, with a huge rucksack behind which we could hardly see her. On top of one of the mountains, Birgit looked with contempt at our sheer delight at the views. She complained, "The rucksack is so heavy and there's nowhere to buy cream cakes." A member of the party, a daughter of the manse, quickly responded in Czech: "You're unbelievably stupid! You deserve a slap in the face! You shouldn't be here at all." I do not know if or how Daniela translated it into German.

I also remember rowing boats on the river Luznice in South Bohemia. The river was so full that it seemed to us that we were floating above the level of the meadows. The floods and warm weather meant that there were swarms of mosquitoes. We were envious of those who could zip up their tents. One day, we borrowed bikes and went for a ride. Daniela clumsily fell off her bike and the lovely trousers she was wearing, and which moreover she had borrowed, got torn. I turned away in pity and in dismissal, as if it did not concern me and I had nothing to do with it. I can still behave like that. Over the years, though, I have lost at least some of my moralistic aloofness.

Chapter 5

A FATEFUL YEAR, AND A YEAR IN AMERICA

The year 1968, the time of the Prague Spring, was a distinct turning point in our student life. The Prague Spring was followed by the arrival of foreign armies. This military invasion was called 'fraternal help' by the intruders.

In the summer of 1968, I completed my examinations in the Faculty of Theology. That August I was in charge of a work camp in Aloysov. Karel Trusina, the Church's youth worker, set aside a couple of days so that he could join us. It was the morning of the 21st August 1968. We had just finished our morning porridge and were getting ready for work. The forest warden arrived as usual. But instead of urging us to set out he said, "There's no hurry today. We're not working. There's a war. The Russians have invaded us. Can't you hear the aircraft?" Indeed, we heard and saw aeroplanes flying west over the mountains. We went back into the common room and sat down leaning against the wooden wall of the hut. Sobbing and weeping was all that was heard in the silence. We realised intensely how the life of society could change very suddenly. In fact it broke down due to the occupation of our country. That experience has made me see in a new light the warnings of the prophets and the hard changes that confronted the people of Israel, the Jews in Europe in the thirties, or Europe and the world after 1939 . . .

We began to think what to do next. As we knew that Prague was being occupied by foreign armies, it was not possible to send the young people from Prague back home. Those from other places could leave, but those from Prague joined Daniela's older sister Lydie, who took them to her cottage on the other side of the mountains. They were living there at the time, because her husband, Pavel, was working nearby doing 'alternative military service'. Daniela and I had to go to

Prague to see the parents of these young people, some as young as fourteen, to tell them that their children were safe.

The train journey was all right, but Prague gave us a shock. We could not find a single address, because people had mixed up street and direction signs in protest against the arrival of the foreign armies. 'Try to find us if you can!' Thus it was not easy for the foreign forces and their helpers to find somebody and detain them. We tried hard to explain what we wanted and why. It was strange not to be able to find our way in our own 'home'. The feeling of fear and danger was strengthened by the deserted streets, an occasional military patrol or a tank . . .

In the following months the opposition to the occupation kept growing until it was gradually subdued and broken by threats and force. At that time, I was the students' representative in the Seminary and a member of the Faculty council meetings. The general atmosphere was very tense. The most radical ones among us appealed to the other students that we should all join the revolutionary Student Union and also openly protest in the streets of Prague. We had to consider how to act and, at the same time, take account of theological and Biblical arguments. In the end, a friend, Vojen Syrovatka, and I went to see the Dean of the Theological Faculty, Professor J. B. Soucek. He listened very carefully to our arguments for the need to take a clear and non-violent stance although it might mean losing one's life. I listened in awe to my favourite teacher: he quietly admitted that he was simply afraid for us.

When I look back at the time before my stay in the United States I am astonished to see that our ordinary days went by in a rather pleasant atmosphere. I still feel the brightness of the fellowship of times long gone. What stands out in my memory is, for example, the worship at the student church of St Martin in the Wall. I sense though that somehow the ordinary times were the exception. Daniela and I, however, had a very special experience in store.

Some of us from the Seminary who finished their studies that year had a chance to study abroad. I used this opportunity and left for Union Theological Seminary in New York in September 1969. I will never forget my departure on the 14th September 1969 – it was the day our daughter Lucie was born. It was impossible for me not to leave. At the time, it was the chance of a lifetime which had been prepared especially for me by Professor J. M. Lochman, who had been a visiting professor at Union Theological Seminary. How strange it is in retrospect that the arrival of our first child seemed to be less significant than a year of study. Lucie was born in Sumperk at 2 pm and the last train I could take to Prague left at the same time. Changing trains at a small station, I heard over the tannoy that I should go to the station master's office. There I received the message that a daughter was born to me; my father-in-law, Rudolf Simek, told me on the telephone.

I do not remember how, a few hours later, after arriving in Prague, I did my packing and left early the next morning. It was too unreal. In our discussions about our future, Daniela and I had a romantic vision that we would all soon meet in New York; we wanted it to be our shared experience. Moreover, I expected that Daniela would support me in my studies and rightly so; the year she spent in Scotland had prepared her for that.

However, my waiting for our reunion was not without tension. Soon after Lucie was born, the state border was closed and all exit visas were declared invalid. I was not prepared to leave my girls on their own in Czechoslovakia, where the situation was becoming rather unfavourable. I was ready to go home but it was not necessary. Daniela was able to obtain new documents and they were both allowed to join me at the end of November. I remember how at JFK airport I flew through all the barriers and welcomed Daniela and Lucie in the international section of the airport. I do not remember, however, how I managed to get back through all the check points.

A year at 'Union' meant for me an intensive study of books and texts, so that I could fulfil the requirements of a Masters Degree programme. Being a member of the Ecumenical Fellows Programme was also a remarkable experience. There were countless meetings, discussions and even disagreements, which we took as coming to terms with the 'big world'. These experiences were extremely pleasant. There was, for example, a weekend retreat 'on ice' with people from Uganda, Korea and Singapore skating for the first time. There were the Monday dinners we took turns to cook; chess games with a Baptist, Carlos Santini, from Spain; discussions with two Brazilians about American power politics . . . One of them was a journalist and would have been imprisoned for his anti-American views in Brazil; he did not live in fear in the United States and could speak freely. The other one, Abivail da Silveira, arrived from Brazil with his wife and children. Later I heard that he became Bishop of the Presbyterian Church in the

Northern Region of Brazil. I also remember table tennis matches with John Miller from Scotland, who was to be my neighbour in Glasgow Presbytery twenty years later.

There was the occasion of a memorial gathering in honour of Professor Josef L. Hromadka. I was asked to speak about his vision of creating a bridge spanning East and West, which should be for people and not herds of cattle.

We saw the Twin Towers grow before our eyes; thirty years on, on 9/11/2001 we watched them fall, taking thousands of innocent lives.

We had a neighbour on the fourth floor in Claremont Avenue, Barbara, a graduate who worked in the library. She found her way to a psychoanalyst, which cost a considerable proportion of her salary. It was something very unusual for us.

The view from our fourth-floor flat gave us a view of the entrance to the Riverside Central Church Offices next to Riverside Church. One day in January we watched as a group of official visitors from all over the world came out of the building and started walking. The first few metres of the pavement were heated and there was no ice. Thereafter we were glad to be hidden high up with our merriment at the view of garments and legs flying into the air, as if they were intentionally sliding on the ice like little children.

My tutor was systematics lecturer Professor Paul Lehmann, but I put my heart into the Old Testament lectures and seminars led by Professor Samuel Terrien and received nourishment from them. He was one of many Europeans who had left the old continent after Hitler came to power. The eastern parts of the United States have been enriched by those who came with their experience from the 'Old World'. I held Professor Terrien in high esteem from the first time I saw him. The year of 1969 was full of student revolt and striving for freedom. It was the beginning of the academic year and student representatives took the seats at the front desk. When Professor Terrien arrived, he was also shown to a seat at the front desk. The representatives started to talk. They tried to explain to us all what the programme for the semester should be like. Professor Terrien listened very intently and eventually said, "So this is your concept of what I should teach. Would it not be better, though, if I tried to teach you what I understand rather than what I am ordered to?" With some hesitation the student representatives agreed. It was like in Exupery's *The Little Prince*: "We order you to teach what you understand."

My short summary of Professor Terrien's lectures at Union comprises three parts encapsulating the points that enriched me the most. The first part carries the title that sums up Terrien's biblical theology, 'The Elusive Presence', which deals with God's presence among us. It is a distinct presence and it can be understood and felt through faith. It cannot be caught, mapped, or, as Professor Soucek liked to call it, 'photographed'. Although it is not possible to capture and keep God's presence, it has been offered to us throughout the whole history of God's people until the arrival of Jesus Christ and thereafter.

The next important point for me is the prophetic recognition that genuine and open acknowledgment and acceptance of God's presence, leading to confession and an authentic attempt to follow him, is ultimately granted only to the remnant of the people. Only they are able to withstand the pressure of corruption, misery and sin and point to God's presence in its fullness.

This relates to the third point: the biblical message, especially in the Old Testament, is full of God's appearance – theophany. From the initial appearances and encounters it progresses and develops until it reaches maturity in the prophets' witness; there God's appearance is no longer accompanied by natural phenomena, or the need for physical appearance. The prophets do not give him a physical likeness as the forefathers needed to do. God's appearance is presented by the Word to the prophet and also by the prophetic Word. It culminates in Jesus Christ, in whom the Old Testament theophany becomes God with us in his Son.

So much for my short reminiscing on the influence exerted on me by the witness of a descendant of old Huguenots, who so distinctly enriched the constellation of the teaching staff at Union Theological Seminary.

What I will always remember is Terrien's pointing out to us that the misery of today lies in the fact that we do not see the dimension of evil in ourselves, around us and above us. Therefore we are not able to appreciate fully the power of God's grace.

During our 'American' year we had the chance to meet new immigrants from Czechoslovakia. It was often a painful experience, because some of them were embittered and disillusioned, probably because of being uprooted and not yet settled in a foreign world. They expressed their disappointment by speaking about their homeland in a derogatory way; having left, they wanted to see their homeland as foreign and even despicable. It was entirely other people's fault and in no way theirs that they had departed. They would say, "Return to Czechoslovakia? No way! Only if I had a huge Cadillac to show the Communists!"

American greed acted as a deterrent to our possible desire to settle in the New World. We took the American experience as a lesson for our future – at home. Too often we were asked if we really meant that we wanted to go back to the concentration camp, and we heard them saying, "You can't go back, not only for your own sakes but because of your daughter who is innocent." But we wanted to return home to the place from which we had been sent out. We owed it to the Faculty, the Church, our families and friends; we also owed it to ourselves. It proved to be difficult to leave. The pressure from some Czech immigrants made us think that we were headed improvidently towards a wall which was solid and insurmountable from the other side. When, after several more years, we were eventually forced to leave home for Scotland, it occurred to me that the dividing wall did not separate only East from West, but also West from East.

I can still see us in America in a romantic summer job at Incarnation Camp, a summer camp at the Bushy Hill Reservoir in Connecticut run by the Episcopal Church. There were three units of girls and three units of boys. I was in charge of one of them. I was the leader of a group of nine-to-eleven-year old boys in five tents, with five boys and a counsellor in each tent. The boys came to stay for two weeks. Some were compliant and good, others wild and naughty. It was interesting to watch how each group, gathered for a fortnight, was like a living organism; it behaved very differently from the previous or following ones. Did the whole group just copy the most influential or active or extreme characters? Is it not like that in society too? It really seems that one or two rebels can disturb or even disrupt the rhythm of life, of pleasant moments, relationships and ambitions. How can we defend ourselves?

Daniela was the 'waterfront counsellor' for pensioners who were part of the big camp although in an independent group. She got the job in the course of our first few days there. We went to the lake and with no hesitation jumped in and swam to the other side. The others just looked on in astonishment and admiration. We were taken for competent swimmers. Only when everybody arrived did we learn how strict the discipline was at the waterfront, so that there would be no accidents. By swimming across the lake without thinking, we showed how ignorant we were. We didn't repeat it.

Apart from the camp for youngsters and pensioners, there was an independent unit for young people over fifteen, called Pioneer Village, on the other side of the reservoir. Andy ruled over all the units. He was a very able leader. He managed to keep the whole camp going. I watched in astonishment how he checked the toilets and bins and did the dirtiest of jobs in his free time. I had to ask him about it. His answer was simple, "Nobody else will do it properly." I admired him.

It was known that I was a theology graduate of a famous Seminary. It must have been for this reason that an Episcopal priest asked me what he should do with communion wafers that were getting mouldy. I suggested throwing them out. He never asked for my advice again.

On one of our days off, a group of us borrowed another counsellor's VW Beetle and drove to a beach near Boston. On our return from the beach we saw that where we had parked there were two or three other red Beetles. We remembered neither our number plate nor the exact spot where we had left ours. I do not remember the happy ending of finding it and getting back to the camp. And there is another story concerning a car. Returning from a swimming excursion, a limousine was put at our disposal. Yes, cars sometimes fall from the sky in America. I was not very happy about it because I was the leader and had to drive in spite of having lost my driving licence. All fourteen of us got into this one vehicle. The car was overloaded and we felt every minor bump on the road, but arrived safely. Naivety and 'innocence' protected us from the consequences of sin.

We left the USA earlier then we had meant to. Our dream to spend the money earned at Incarnation Camp on a journey across the States was not fulfilled. We received a letter from the Synodal Council of the Evangelical Church of Czech Brethren in Prague demanding that we should return by the end of August, so that I would be able to start working in my first congregation at the beginning of the school year.

Chapter 6

BACK TO CZECHOSLOVAKIA: MINISTRY IN TELECI

On our return to Czechoslovakia, we did not find it to be a concentration camp as some of the immigrants in the USA had imagined. It was different from the time of Stalinism in the fifties. Normalisation in the occupied Czechoslovakia appeared to be proceeding gradually and only later did we realise that the network of oppression and surveillance was very dense.[1] Our own situation was very different from that described by the Synodal Council when they asked me to return from the USA as soon as possible: I could not start work immediately. Frustration crept in.

First it was Comrade Jonas, the regional government clerk supervising churches, who held our fate in his hands. He refused to grant a licence to work as a minister to a man who 'came from his American provider' and who did not agree with the 'fraternal help of the friendly armies'.

A CV had to contain the applicant's stance towards August 1968 events. What follows is a part of my CV:

> . . . My stance towards the events of August 1968 is similar to my stance towards all other interventions where force is used. As a Christian I oppose the use of force as a means of solving a conflict or problem in the world. Knowing the teachings of the Gospels, I profess a way of powerlessness and non-violence, love and peace for all. I have accepted the teaching of Petr Chelcicky, who in the 15th century went

---

1 For details of the 'Samota' document on Tomas Bisek, see Appendix 1. Samota translates literally as 'seclusion' (the manse in Teleci was in a remote place, which is the translation given in Appendix 1), an example of the odd titles or codes given to each of the many files kept by State Security on people they wanted to monitor.

as far as to criticise the Hussite revolt and the use of force even in self-defence. I admire the ideas of Leo Tolstoy in his writings, although his totally peaceful way may be seen as naïve. I would like to understand better the thinking of Mahatma Ghandi in his way of peaceful protest in India. One of the heroes of today for me is Dr Martin Luther King, the campaigner for the rights for black people in the USA, who with his peaceful actions created a truly revolutionary situation and gave rise to a revolutionary movement. I am strongly convinced and instructed through the study of history that the use of force produces destruction, malice and hatred; nobody benefits, neither the victims nor the perpetrators. I am afraid that in this respect I can criticise all governments who very readily breach the UN Charter, which they themselves proposed, agreed on and signed . . .

For the three of us it meant constantly extending our stay with Daniela's parents in a one-bedroom flat. There were no squabbles thanks to the good will of her parents. "You returned from a country with which there is normally only one-way traffic", said Mr Sobotka, the librarian at the Faculty of Theology. Perhaps we were a bit naive in expecting to be allowed to begin work straight away. Now we feel we have gathered some experience in waiting. But we do not think we can give much advice on how to avoid it, because things just happen in their own time.

The Synodal Senior at that time, Vaclav Kejr, played his part in ending our provisional status. He had also returned from the USA, although it was before World War II. He added his argument, "Mr Bisek had been properly sent to study abroad and he also returned as required. Protesting against the use of power is compatible with the stance of the church".

Mr Kejr was successful in his plea, though not with Comrade Jonas. It was the Ministry of Culture that granted my licence and, consequently, I was allowed to go to the congregation in the village of Teleci, where the Synodal Council thought I should start. Our transition from the skyscrapers of Manhattan to a village of six hundred people in the Bohemian Uplands began. During the year in America we had grown used to looking up the walls of buildings several hundred feet high and scraping the skies. At home we could see all around and saw meadows, woods and cottages scattered on the slopes on both sides of a road which climbed for five kilometres up to Lucky Hill. Once I got stuck in my car in a snowdrift on this hill when I was going to see somebody. The postman happened to be walking past. He put down his bag with the post and helped me to get back onto the road. After this experience, I always relied on my skis whenever there was snow.

I remember my first time in Teleci, my future congregation. I visited the session clerk Josef Dvorak in house number twenty six for the first time. I ate scrambled eggs with home-made bread, drank coffee with five lumps of sugar and listened to the accent of the Bohemian Uplands. Then the deputy clerk, Mr Lamplot, took me in his tractor to the station four miles away. The cold air of an evening in late autumn and the journey in the open tractor meant that my hands and feet gradually got very cold. I could feel a pain in my ear. I was afraid I would suffer a recurrence of the inflammation of my middle ear that had plagued me when I was younger.

However, in autumn 1970, I was very happy to receive a call to preach as sole nominee in Teleci. The interim Moderator and a friend of mine, Bohdan Pivonka, picked me up at the station and took me to Teleci where I was to preach. Bohdan was excited that I might be one of his neighbours and said, "I'll show you what we have here, Tomas." He stopped the car, got out and said, "Wait a minute." After a short while he returned with an armful of wild edible mushrooms. I did not want to be fooled and I said, "You set that up yesterday."

"OK, let's do it again", he said and crossed the road and disappeared into the woods. In a little while he was back with another armful of mushrooms and a broad smile. He laughed when I said, "I would not have expected you to set it up on both sides of the road!"

Then I had to undergo the pressure of conducting the Sunday service in a place I did not know and in an unusual situation. The Session deliberated and I waited for their verdict. Bohdan came out and said, "So you've just been accepted as their minister, boy. Congratulations!" I joined the meeting and expressed my thanks and my hope that the Almighty would be gracious to us.

I find it interesting that I have never failed to thank God for the possibility of serving in the church. I am also grateful that preachers of the Word are allowed to work with different congregations, as for example were Bohdan and I: first both of us in the Bohemian Uplands, then Bohdan in Prague and I in Glasgow, later he in the prison chaplaincy and I in Prague. The fact that ministers of religion can do their work is a manifestation, in the first place, of God's extraordinary favour, but also of the good will of society yesterday and today, though they often do not realise it. Are we worthy of the opportunity? I reflect on the power of the creative Spirit, which allows unprepared, imperfect and failing fellows like us to set out on a journey of service. I was reminded of this in a couple of ways a few months after I started work in Teleci.

First, there was an extraordinarily frank statement made by 'Uncle' Trnka, an elder of the congregation, "I tell you, Mr Bisek, I voted for you only because you came from America". I let it go without a comment or question. The next thing happened on the hillside opposite the manse. A few church members were helping to get in a supply of wood for the manse. Two elders were chopping off branches close to one another and chatting:

"Joseph, what do you think we'll get for this?"

"Well, bugger-all, Tony! A treasure in heaven."

I was standing too near to pretend not to have heard it. And I was also well aware that the two had not realised it. Still laughing they noticed me and I chipped in, "But the treasure will count for a lot". They did not stop laughing.

We were in the manse yard. 'Uncle' Lamplot, the father of Tony, who later became the session clerk of the congregation, was standing at the circular saw and feeding in the blocks I was handing to him. He warned me several times, "Don't you ever go any closer, Mr Bisek. You have no idea what a saw can do!" Twelve years later I was in the forest using a chainsaw. I could not have got any closer to it, but 'Uncle' Lamplot did not see it. He was no longer among the living. I remember him with gratitude.

TOMAS WITH HIS FATHER AND BROTHERS

Finally, in November 1970 we moved into the refurbished manse in Teleci and were allowed to begin our life there. I looked out of the manse windows and counted the cottages I could see. The fingers of one hand were enough. I felt somehow uneasy. What had we done that we were so lost? Though on reflection, how could we think we were lost? For when I thought back to it a few years later, I knew I could feel the rhythm of the village at that time: "The family in number forty five are just having lunch. Naca is coming home from the fields. The children are leaving the school. Somebody is watering a grave in the cemetery behind the church and so we have no running water for a while." I could see living faces through the walls, I imagined their gestures and I felt their hard, calloused hands . . .

From my pastoral life in Teleci I remember in particular two funerals. At one of these, the funeral service at the house of mourning was over. The house was on a hill overlooking the village. The procession of mourners that followed the horse-drawn hearse was slowly descending to the village. I was walking in my preaching gown right behind the hearse and, as we were going down, I had time to think and look at the village from my peculiar position. All of a sudden a thought flashed through my mind: I was not sure which name I had used at the house. Did I say Frantisek Swift? Or did I say Frantisek Sparrow? Do swift and sparrow fly in the same way? I kept talking to myself, "Sparrow? Swift? No, Swift! How do I have it in my notes? – Swift. So it's ok! What's ok? Nothing's ok. Perhaps I already made a mistake when preparing for the burial. Did I check in the register? No, I didn't!" Then in despair I told myself, "You have to use the same name as at the house. Ok, so it's Swift!!" The procession was near the church now. We were walking past the manse and I saw our children hanging over the fence. The oldest, Lucie, called out loudly in the most innocent voice, "Hiya, Daddy!" I tried to pretend I didn't see the children and walked by in a dignified manner, as the circumstances demanded. But I made a face at them and the more I made a face, the more they smiled and waved to me.

Only years later, the children told me that they managed to do a lot of things when there were funerals in Teleci. In their curiosity they even managed to open the lid of a coffin that had been brought into the church too early. And at the cemetery they "gave the poor what they had taken from the rich". Yes, they took flowers and plants from one grave and put them on another to install social justice in the cemetery. Oh, children, children!

I will conclude my memories of the peculiar funeral procession with this finding: I was relieved to find that it was 'Swift' in the congregational register.

The story of the second funeral came from Milos, a man from a village that lies over the hill from Teleci. There was a burial taking place. It was an unusually civic or even political burial. The local Party Chairman had died. Just like his 'colleague' in Teleci, he had never been accepted by the people in the village. This was, in fact, what the Party desired, because then it was easier for them to manipulate and supervise. The Party Chairman was able to cause tensions or disrupt the people's unity as necessary.

Milos was walking past the cemetery and heard somebody concluding the burial oration. Suddenly a voice called over the wall, "Milos, we need your help! There aren't enough of us to lower the coffin into the grave". Yes, there were not enough mourners. They had to invite a passer-by, a Good Samaritan, not because of a person who had been left half dead but because of a neighbour who had been rejected and left utterly alone thanks to Party politics. I don't think that Milos would ever forget that occasion.

For me as a novice pastor, the battle for the Sunday service began. The whole village gathered at funerals but only a handful came to church. Brother Dvorak tried to cheer me up: "The church used to be full before the war and even in the fifties. Being an elder meant a social status. But how many people really believed? Only a few, like today."

I did not accept his consolation. Moreover, I was a big-headed young fellow. At a Presbytery meeting, when I was to account for the first year of my ministry, I told them what I thought: I said openly that I saw the end of the congregation in Teleci. "Have a look at the figures for the last few years and you'll see how inevitable the end is."

It was nonsense. The movement and changes in a congregation depend to a great extent on the living and inspiring Word, which sometimes comes in a human voice. Sometimes it comes in the work of hands and minds. Sometimes it comes in the lives of witnesses. Sometimes, beyond our understanding, the breath of the Spirit gives life to totally dry bones.

Sociological data and demographic prognosis can help us to understand, but sometimes they can also obscure the truth. All depends on the One who has our congregations in his hand. It also depends on the life of each and every one of us: whether we want to live as witnesses of Christ. Then what we think and expect on the basis of our own experience is no longer valid. God makes all things new. He changes everything.

In our everyday life in Teleci we became gradually aware of a tangible blessing from above. Our son Lukas arrived in 1971. He was the only one of our babies who I was allowed to see immediately after he was born. It was on a Sunday at the end of March. There was an elders' conference in Brno and I had been asked to talk at it about my studies in the States. I was still at the conference when I got the news that the baby would not be long. I drove as fast as I could straight to the maternity hospital in Policka and arrived at exactly the right moment. My open mouth defeated the midwives and they showed me my baby son in the arms of a nurse. I could even give Daniela a wave! Why only a wave? I was extremely fortunate to be allowed as much. It was an unbelievable exception.[2] How different it was from the experience of our son-in-law, Samuel. He was present at the birth of all his children in Scotland.

The following year Ester was born to us. She had to cope with the fact that the umbilical cord was wound round her tiny neck. The precarious nature of the birth of a new life started to dawn on us. The most dramatic was the birth of our youngest, Benjamin, in 1974. After two days, the amniotic fluid had disappeared and the doctors and midwives started to race around the mother. Then the information that Daniela had to cope with came, and the nurse said, "We don't have to hurry any more. It's too late. I can't hear the baby's heartbeat . . ." But the doctor was able to act and Benjamin was helped to enter the world. I realised that it was often difficult for hospital staff to be considerate and tactful.

It goes without saying that the arrival of two girls and two boys one after the other: a girl, a boy, a girl and a boy, four healthy children, is a fascinating thing for parents. We both have three siblings. Daniela has two sisters and a brother, I have two brothers and a sister. Our four children meant Daniela had to abandon her vision of studying English and Russian at the Faculty of Education in Prague, where she had been accepted. She never managed to enrol.

At the start of my ministry, there were two pressing questions: what would it be like for an unconfident person from Prague living and working in a village? In my time there were no placements with experienced ministers and no probationers. And would I be able to begin in the right way?

---

2 Fathers were not allowed in the maternity wards until the nineties; not even to visit.

Chapter 7

THE CHURCH, GOVERNMENT OFFICIALS AND RISING TENSION

The Moderator of the Presbytery came to see me. I told him that I did not know how I should go about visiting people. "What does a pastoral visit mean?" I asked. I got this reply: "You'll soon find out yourself, boy. The important thing is to be able to fill out the quarterly reports, so that you'll have no difficulties with the government officials." After a number of years in a congregation, the Moderator had a lot of experience with tricky government officials. He knew well that there would be difficulties. However in my case, these, when they came, did not concern quarterly reports.

Later, I saw things clearly: the prime purpose of government officials supervising churches at the time of the suppression of 'religiosity' was to divert ministers from their work. The government clerk was to sabotage those activities that 'deepened and stimulated religiosity', as he would say himself. Therefore we were presented with difficulties which could be eliminated only if we succumbed to government pressure, fully complied and simply marked time.

It was unsettling to see the variety of reactions among my colleagues to the pressure from the government. The ministers in our Presbytery seemed to be divided into two groups. One was the group of older ministers who remembered the fifties, when the churches had been dealt with especially harshly. These senior colleagues had gathered experience which we, the novices, did not have. They, the experienced ones, saw our conduct towards government officials as improper and our problems as trivial. In their view, we could not prevail and it was paramount to reach a *modus vivendi*, which meant, in fact, tolerating our circumscribed existence.

The government officials found the split in our ranks opportune. They targeted us, the 'inexperienced' ones, with their critical comments and prepared sanctions in advance. They justified this on the grounds that it was we who found it difficult to accept their suggestions, requests and requirements. We on the other hand saw their actions as an attempt to show us that we had to conform.

Once, a district government clerk was at a ministers' meeting in one of our congregations. He presented his request: "And now, gentlemen, give me your car registration numbers." All our senior colleagues obliged with no hesitation. Then it was our turn. One after another refused the request, pointing out that the clerk had the numbers already anyway or that he could copy them from the cars parked outside. He left the meeting indignant, uttering warnings and threats.

A heated discussion ensued among the ministers. The ones who had complied with the request argued that, "It makes absolutely no sense not to go along with such a simple demand which in fact only amounted to writing down some numbers. He probably needs to show that he is doing something and this is only an attempt to show that he is in control. Making an issue of this pettiness only aggravates your relationship with the authorities." We, on the other hand, maintained that the district clerk's request had not been justified, because he did not come from the State Security and it was not within his remit of supervising the church. He had tried to make us obey and had overstepped the limits to what he could request from us. "Where are the limits to what he will demand tomorrow?" someone asked. In fact, the real problem lay within our own ranks. We were not able to unite and target the real source of our oppression, but were being divided by an artificial issue which the clerk so cleverly brought up. Was this not clear evidence of the despotism with which the authorities were pursuing us? It started with the car registration numbers, then followed the prohibition of visits from abroad, later visits in general and, finally, being obliged to report our own movements.

Indeed, it went too far. The noose was getting tighter. Did it seem that what was happening was confusing and inconsistent? It was in essence sheer despotism. The issues were presented to us in a haphazard manner, requesting compliance one day and servility the next. What is my view then of how a body of ministers can maintain solidarity in the face of pressure from the authorities? I do not think that in such a situation different points of view about how to cope with more powerful and unjust adversaries are a problem in themselves. Our problem was that we were not able to face and accept our differences. Therefore the division originated on the inside; among us. The community of those who should have supported one another, and even wanted to do so, started to disintegrate.

I remember in this connection a further encounter, or rather a non-encounter, in Teleci with my former seminary teacher Milan Opocensky, with whom I had had an uncomfortable relationship in Prague. One Saturday night, my colleague Mila from a neighbouring parish phoned, "We have a guest in our congregation, Brother Opocensky. He says he would like to see you."

"Come over," I replied.

"OK, tomorrow after lunch," was the arrangement.

TELECI MANSE

On Sunday, we all waited in front of the manse. There was fresh snow on the ground and our children were tobogganing. A car passed. Mila waved to us. The car disappeared. We did not understand. Mila phoned in the evening, "I am very sorry. I don't understand it either. Milan was driving and just before we reached your house he said that there wasn't enough time; he would be late and would rather drive straight home."

I noticed traces of impatience on my own part right at the beginning of my years in the Presbytery. One of the saddest moments was a conversation when we tried to force the Moderator of the Presbytery to acknowledge the brutality of the government and the dirty work of the government officials supervising churches. He could not accept it, perhaps because of his role as Moderator and also because of his concern for us, which we did not understand. The damage caused was permanent. I am afraid that we contributed to his having a feeling of isolation, which I was not able to see at that time.

I can now see how impatient I was, and how we had a certainty that we were simply right. Did subsequent developments confirm this? Or did our attitudes rather show that we were not able to acknowledge and admit our many failures and therefore we lost our sharpness of vision and our understanding of the detail of people's lives? We failed to see what was perhaps the basis of what others lived for, although we were supposed to share our lives with them.

Going to the village school and teaching religion in class was completely new to me; in Prague it had been long forgotten. In many ways the school environment was not conducive to it. The normal teaching process is different from sharing faith and creed. Moreover, schooling involved an active denial of religion. A head teacher, responsible for setting the rules for religious classes, was under pressure to prove that religiosity at the school was declining. Certainly the environment of manses or church buildings would have been much more appropriate for us. However, if we had moved religious classes from schools to church buildings, the pressure would have shifted in that direction as well, so that children would not have been able to attend.

The pressure was significant. I remember when the parents of children enrolled for religious classes were summoned before the local council in Teleci and informed that religious classes opposed the 'world scientific view'. "Your children are exposed to obscurantism and it is very important that you withdraw your child from the religious class. Otherwise there may be no possibility for your bright offspring to pursue further study," the parents were told.

It seemed obvious to me that the official ideology was elevated to the level of a science, and that state power was felt to be more powerful than truth. The result of the parents being threatened by the local council was an atmosphere of uncertainty and fear. Most of the families in Teleci had had a hard time of it when collectivization was being imposed; the harmony between them and nature seemed to have been disturbed, because the Stalinist era trampled on their lifestyle. Many of them had lost their natural self-confidence and self-esteem. All the wisdom gained over generations was put in question.

A few farmers did not join the cooperative farming. Their children, however, were taken away from their parents' influence so that they would be 'properly re-educated'.

I felt compelled to write a protest against the parents being threatened. The regional clerk supervising churches responded that schools were not in his remit and he added that the percentage of ministers' children studying at university was high above the average; "So what are you complaining about?" The clerk used political rhetoric to try to distract me from the actual issue and, at the same time, he reminded me that to have a child studying at a specialised secondary school or university was a privilege for both the parents and the child. It should make them grateful.

My growing opposition towards the hostile regime was still being kept out of the house at the beginning of the seventies. Our life was blissful, filled with caring for our four healthy, lively and thriving children. The opportunity for their activities at that age was broad: from the manse and church, through the graveyard and into the fields, meadows and woods all around.

Having been brought up in town and city, we resisted, perhaps too strongly, the suggestions that we should keep a goat, or at least rabbits, so that we would always have some meat on our table. Cats were the only pets that kept coming to find a home with us. Next door to the manse was a byre where bulls were kept. The neighbours tending the bulls also had hens and geese. There were plenty of animals in the village. The meagre pay I had was generously supplemented by the members of the congregation and other friendly folk. We were given eggs most often; at Easter and Christmas we regularly received fowl and when a pig was slaughtered, the gift often consisted of several bags with meat, white and black pudding, soup and even pig's blood. There was also a scheme of financial help from the Swiss Church, through which ministers' families were supported by individuals or congregations. We enjoyed the friendly ties that developed with the Swiss and that have not ended yet. I hope I can say also for Daniela, who did the housekeeping, that we never felt any lack of material things.

However the pleasant rural life we led was being more and more disturbed, not only by the pressure of 'normalisation' of the Russia-inspired regime, which was generally felt in the village, but also by a tangible interest of the State Security in me as someone who had returned from the USA.

In 1977 Alastair Hulbert from Scotland took over as Secretary of the WSCF in Geneva. Alastair was Fiona Williams' boyfriend when she studied at our Faculty in Prague in 1966-67 and stayed in the Seminary in the room next to Daniela's and mine. It was the first year of our married life. We used to spend a lot of time with Fiona. Consequently, she arranged for Daniela to spend the following year in Scotland as an au-pair girl and to learn English.

On his appointment as Europe Secretary of the WSCF, Alastair got a visa and came to Prague. Prior to his coming he arranged through a friend that we would meet. So Daniela and I met Alastair, sure that no other person knew about this meeting. Alastair was very much interested in the situation of our Evangelical Church of Czech Brethren. There were a few ministers whose licences to work had already been withdrawn by the government clerks. How would the Synodal Council, the Church Headquarters, react? What would be the situation in the congregations? We discussed these matters.

Several weeks passed before I was summoned for one of a series of interrogations by the State Security. Only at the end of the day was the question which I had felt might come asked: "Mr Hulbert travels all over Europe and talks to students from the western countries about the persecution of the churches here. We know, Mr Bisek, that he has information from you!" I did not reply and wondered if Alastair had mentioned me as the source.

As a result, Alastair was refused a visa to visit Czechoslovakia for many years. We met only in Scotland where our family arrived in 1985, as the result of action by the State Security called 'clearance' which meant that about one hundred people or families were earmarked for expulsion from the country. Only then did I learn that Alastair had written a short report on his visit in 1977 which he had circulated confidentially to a small group of friends. Many years later, when I was finishing writing my memoirs, he told me that he had given my name as the source of the information in the report he had written about the situation of the church, and that he had also mentioned our meeting to Mr Opocensky. He believed Opocensky was his friend and was staying with him at the time. Who knows where the breach of confidentiality happened?

State Security interest in me grew rather dramatically after a private meeting with colleagues and former fellow-students at one of our manses. A government official supervising churches suddenly and unexpectedly appeared and declared our meeting illegal. Then he called the police who checked our papers, wrote down our particulars and made us leave. The meeting was, according to them, illegal because we had not asked for permission to meet and had not given the reason for our meeting. Our explanation that it was an informal meeting of friends was not accepted as an excuse. I sat down and wrote a letter to the regional clerk and to the Synodal Council. The gist of the letter was a defence of the right of friends to hold an informal meeting at a manse. The host, Petr Brodsky, and I received letters from the regional clerk where our 'anti-socialist and treasonous' attitudes were exposed. Consequently, Petr's licence to work as a minister in the local congregation was revoked by the government clerk and he was forced to move to a congregation in a far corner of south east Moravia, about two hundred kilometres away. My punishment was a reduced stipend, from eleven hundred to nine hundred Crowns a month. Ironically enough, the child benefit we received for our four children was sixteen hundred Crowns a month.

This informal meeting of friends became the first in a line of regular gatherings where we met with younger and older colleagues and discussed our problems – not only challenges within our congregations, but also problems with the authorities. The ministers who had already had their licences revoked and had manual jobs, usually as stokers, used to come too. They were not allowed to attend any church conferences and official meetings by order of the Synodal Council, due to the pressure from the authorities.

The tension grew, not only due to the pressure exerted on us by the government, but also because we felt disillusioned by the way the regime dealt with people in general: how they kept restricting contacts with people from abroad, how they assumed that they had the right to determine what the relationships between church members, colleagues in ministry and friends should be like. The more the scope of church activities was restricted, the more we felt that it was necessary to confront the situation. The colleagues who had challenged the authorities, either overtly or inadvertently, and were already without their licences, were our role models.

In retrospect I realise that I gave up my anonymity and decided to face being an outcast when the State Security started summoning me for questioning. It began after the first meeting with fellow-ministers and it lasted three days. Later the interrogations became more or less regular throughout the years. The following conversation was the beginning of a bizarre dialogue which stretched over a long period and was interrupted by weeks of waiting apprehensively to see whether I was getting another 'visit': two State Security men arriving early in the morning and taking me away, usually to Svitavy, a town fifteen miles away, to the police station. After weeks and months of it I could see the pattern of our dialogues which I, in fact, initiated and which certainly made the sessions considerably longer. It went something like this:

"What are your neighbours like?" I would ask.

"Normal," replied Mr Tucek. "What do you mean? What should they be like?"

"I'm just interested in what you do in your free time and how your neighbours see you," I would go on.

After a while Mr Tucek said, "Mr Bisek, we're just like anyone else."

I did not say anything and after a while I was given an unexpected explanation:

"Since you ask, Mr Bisek, tell us, is there anything unusual about us?"

"Why are you asking that question?" I asked.

"Look, once we were working in your Prague . . ." (by saying 'your Prague' they implied that they knew about my past; they liked to mention a few snippets from one's life, sometimes incredibly detailed, so that one would think that they were omniscient), "and we went to a restaurant to get something to eat. A waiter asked, 'What will you have, comrades?'" (i.e. party members).

They were clearly waiting for a response, so I said, "Well, you are comrades, aren't you?" They reacted immediately, "But that's not the way to address guests in a restaurant, is it? Do we look different from others?" In my mind I laughed but did not say anything. It was clear to me that the waiter was experienced and could smell the State Security out. I also realised that I had got a clear answer to my question as to how supporters of an oppressive government, dutiful flunkies as they were, felt amongst 'normal' people.

Chapter 8

CHARTER 77

In the course of the seventies we realised that those 'normal' people were well aware that the state of affairs was getting more and more precarious and that the huge gulf between the new regime and the period of the Prague Spring in 1968 was deepening. The Prague Spring was a short period of 'socialism with a human face', as it was called. It could be seen as a symbolic handshake between the Communist reformer Alexander Dubcek and the Protestant theologian Josef Lukl Hromadka. Hromadka had been encouraging Christians in Czechoslovakia to adopt a positive stance towards the Communist coup of 1948. He had been led to this approach by his disappointment with the Munich Agreement in 1938, when the western democracies proved themselves unreliable, and he also saw that they were unable to solve the problem of growing social inequality. All this had led Hromadka to see the Russian October Revolution of 1917 as a positive attempt to solve social problems by force and to create a so-called 'classless society'. Hromadka had been calling for the acceptance of this challenge in the hope that it might be possible to humanise it.

Here I am reminded of a public discussion I had on this theme with a representative of the Scottish Communist Party in the Pearce Institute in Glasgow at the end of the eighties. A secondary school teacher who was also an erudite historian gave the audience strong arguments that there was hope for humankind in an uprising of the proletariat and the establishment of a just society. In my answer I pointed to our Czech experience of great ideals being perverted and often twisted into the opposite by corrupt people. I also said that it wasn't possible either to reform people fully or to prepare them for real and full justice. My opponent presented evidence that in history such plans and visions had always been perverted. But, he continued, if we knew how to use our experience and disappointments correctly, we could still reach our goal. I could not retreat from my argument that this was a utopia, although nevertheless it was also the ultimate expectation of my own faith.

For me this hope has always been based on the description of a miracle recorded in the Bible in the book of Acts. I quote: "All the believers continued together in close fellowship and shared their belongings with one another. They would sell their property and possessions, and distribute the money among all, according to what each one needed. Day after day they met as a group in the Temple, and they had their meals together in their homes, eating with glad and humble hearts" (Acts 2:44-46). But did Hromadka not envisage the implementation of this utopia on earth far too easily when he described the role of Christians as being to bring Christ's spirit of peace and reconciliation into the turmoil imposed by violent revolutions? Surely he often had to turn a blind eye to the atrocities committed in the name of social justice. It is terrible to hear the popular saying: "You can't make an omelette without breaking eggs." He must have felt many a tension and disappointment, if not disillusionment, when he saw all the violence and perverse actions committed in the name of social justice. It is difficult not to feel that he may have been taken advantage of on a number of occasions.

Today, we can see that the Christian Peace Conference, created as a meeting place for positive and peaceful currents from East and West, was riddled with police place-men serving Moscow's power politics. Did Hromadka have to turn a blind eye to that? This was a question in many people's minds, and later they even asked it out loud. It was not until twenty years after the Communist Coup that Hromadka could see a possible dawning of his vision during the reforms in the spring of 1968.

The men in power in Moscow, however, felt that there was danger looming in the Prague Spring. The spirit of revival and transparency threatened their power. They saw how quickly Dubcek's controlled 'thaw' was changing into a new demand from the grassroots. People wanted the end of the rule of the Communist Party and the beginning of real democracy in a free Czechoslovakia. The tanks of the so-called friendly armies rolling in on 21st August 1968 and the repression that followed put an end to that extraordinary vision. 'Normalization' began and all initiatives that seemed to be potentially dangerous were gradually and deliberately suppressed. The slowness of the process allowed the Kremlin's henchmen to devise a comprehensive network of repression to secure their domination. The most ambitious General Secretary of the Communist Party and President of the country, Gustav Husak, served the purpose very well. The gradual and ever wider repression probably helped a tentative resistance to emerge.

It did not take long before people were questioned and imprisoned because they publicly pointed out where freedom and democracy were being surreptitiously suppressed. They tried to encourage their fellow-citizens to use their civic freedom at the first elections after the Prague Spring. The flyers they had been distributing, which called for freedom and responsibility in decision-making, were earmarked as being anti-state and the distributors were imprisoned. Milos Rejchrt, a minister of the church, called for the church to leave the pro-regime Christian Peace Conference. It was the beginning of ministers having their state licences rescinded. There were also others who were being punished for their open and pointed critique of the situation. Of course, not only church people were being persecuted. There were those who were convinced that it was necessary to form alliances in order to defend the right to live in freedom.

During this dramatic flow of events, in our rural isolation we did not at first see that, unknowingly and quite independently, we were becoming part of the growing movement against the totalitarian regime. The Husak government's bold display of a human face to the world led to signing the Helsinki Treaty of Human Rights in 1976. But, as usual, those in power assumed that nothing, not even a supposedly binding signature, could curtail their power to suppress everything that makes a person a complete human being responsible for their own words and deeds. The government cynically continued to suppress the basic human rights and freedoms allegedly guaranteed by the Treaty. And it was exactly this that became a signal for the opposition to come out into the open.

I remember an incident typical of the conflict in people's thoughts and actions caused by the pressure to conform and blindly obey. Vaclav Havel described how he had met a film director friend and told him about his anguish at the unjust trial of a group of young musicians. As a deterrent to others, apparently, they had been given a prison sentence for singing their own songs without a licence. "And I", Havel told his friend, "am walking free because I'm well-known. You see? It's intolerable?!" To change the subject, his friend replied after a while, "And, how are you otherwise?" At this moment Havel realised that there was no 'otherwise'

– he couldn't go on pretending that the fate of young musicians and other persecuted people did not concern him. There were two of my fellow theology students among the musicians, Vratislav Brabenec and Svatopluk Karasek. With some others I managed to get into the corridor in the court building at the time of the trial. We weren't allowed to attend the proceedings, but we saw our friends being led away in handcuffs and we could only wave to them.

Such events, disenchantment, disappointments, frustration, fear, uncertainty, and always new arbitrary rules, threats and punishments led a group of alert people to an undaunted opposition. With their consciences aroused they decided to support the government in the task of fulfilling the Helsinki Treaty. And so the founding document of Charter 77 came into existence. The text, nearly four pages long, finishes with this sentence: "We believe that Charter 77 will contribute towards all citizens in Czechoslovakia working and living as free people. 1. 1. 1977." Many other documents followed until 1989, often several in a month, as Chartists endeavoured to point out various iniquities in policies which affected people's lives. Those involved knew that in the atmosphere of oppression and general deception they could expect only a hate-filled response.

They were right in their premonitions. Those in power did not accept their offer to support the government in the pledge to respect human rights as a friendly gesture but as an attempt to attack communist ideals. Their reaction was not only immediate and hate-filled, but also underhand and dishonest. The public were not to know the real content of the critics' declaration. Instead, a fierce campaign against the first signatories was unleashed. The text of Charter 77 was not made officially public until the Velvet Revolution in 1989.

One of the first spokespersons and the spiritual leader of Charter 77 was a philosopher, Professor Jan Patocka. He explained to us that the values which Charter 77 presented were the basic values if a person was to live responsibly and in freedom and it was not possible to surrender them. As our government had signed the human rights declaration, and so demonstrated that human dignity and freedom were to be preserved, then it was necessary to be ready to make sacrifices to make them a reality. Both Jan Patocka and Vaclav Havel said clearly that there are values which are worthy of our suffering. One cannot live without them; one can only vegetate miserably.

Jan Patocka was internationally known as a philosopher in spite of living in seclusion for years. He was like a thorn in the government's flesh and therefore was subjected to an interrogation lasting eleven hours after his meeting with the Dutch Minister of Foreign Affairs in the first stormy months of Charter 77. The interrogation ended with Patocka suffering a heart attack. He died in hospital at the age of seventy, never regaining consciousness, on 13th March 1977. We all saw clearly that the regime could be extremely ruthless. But the first signatories succeeded in disturbing the apathy and lethargy of others. The first document of Charter 77 was circulated widely despite the government's campaign against it and in spite of signatories and sympathisers being persecuted and ostracized. Their number kept slowly growing.

How did Daniela and I decide to sign Charter 77? The last push for us to exit *chronos*, the time that runs, flows and ticks away incessantly, and enter *kairos*, the moment of opportunity or the critical time set apart, came when we visited my colleagues and our friends, Jana and Pavel, in their manse in the village of Horni Dubenky. There we saw and read the initial Charter 77 Document and the names of the first signatories, about one hundred and forty of them. Among them were people we knew well and who were already in trouble: our colleagues whose licences had been revoked. Had they signed the document because they had nothing to lose? Certainly not! At least we did not perceive it that way. Quite the contrary, in spite of suffering under despotism they had the courage to point at instances where the law was being broken. We all knew that those in power threatened and punished and, at the same time, never stopped offering a variety of inducements.

Psychological intimidation thrived and took the form of showing the victim that those in power could sometimes deliver a kick and sometimes a smile. The purpose was to bring a person to obedience by both fear and an expectation of reward. Suppression was directed not only at religion but at any opposition in general, be it spiritual independence or free creativity. It was necessary to show solidarity when one saw how the regime often divided, separated, silenced and suppressed people who were weak and marginalised. Should we not stop hiding away in the face of pressure, while feeling ashamed and guilty because we had no regard for those being harassed partly on our behalf?

This is how a completely new, unexpected and hardly believable chapter opened in our family's life. It began by trying gradually to find our own dignity. After plucking up one's courage to make a personal decision and showing one's own position, a space for dignity opens: we should remain ourselves and stick to what we believe and, at the same time, recognise what our responsibility is: to discern what we can agree with and what we should reject. We should evaluate, choose, accept or refuse when we look for truth, justice and peace.

Another aspect of our new life was striking: we found a new community. Charter 77 opened up in us a willingness to understand the tensions and different orientations in individuals and groups. Suddenly, we were on a journey together with new friends, together seeking new ways, together under pressure and in danger, but also in hope and joy. Our manse in a small village in the Bohemian Uplands became a place where signatories and their friends kept coming. Most of them were from Prague, but some were also from Brno and other places.

Once a State Security man, soon to retire, described to me our new situation, "You, Mr Bisek, think that you are the follower of Mr Kadlec, who was the minister in your congregation during the Second World War. In his time, the opponents of Nazism used to find shelter in the manse. They even called it the 'Hotel'. And you think that you are following in his footsteps. You're very wrong! Mr Kadlec opposed Nazism. And you? You are serving those who have betrayed the working class, who cannot comprehend the inevitability of our journey towards Communism, which is the only just and right order in society. You'll be really very sorry if you don't stop. And do you think the working class doesn't mind waiting before its hard fist hits those who are in their way? Remember, you have a family. What say do your children have over your activities? You remind me of the fifties, when collectivisation took place. There was the farmer, his wife and their children, all lined up. I felt very sorry for him, but he had to be imprisoned for his treasonous activities. You will end up like him!"

That was in the early days of my enforced contacts with the State Security. Soon I was in the hands of a younger generation. They never bothered to be as ideological as their older colleague was. I do not think they knew how and they probably did not see any need for it. Without hesitation they would show me how I would be ground to nothing between their two palms which were, in fact, millstones. These moments were special for me for I strangely felt the presence of a very different protective power. However, very regularly, when I had left the musty police room and was outside, in the fresh air, I had a strong feeling of frustration and loss: I had just endured a hopeless waste of time. These interrogations were times of having to deal with absurd suspicions, threats and boasting, while at other times I was expected to be pliable and servile. Would my best tactic be to prevaricate? But why should I have to do that? Or should I try to overpower them, or convince them – or to convict them?

"It is we who're asking the questions here, Mr Bisek," they would say whenever they felt it was necessary. I kept asking them questions nevertheless and sometimes I even received answers. A clear understanding would come to me from Matthew's Gospel: ". . . and then the devil left Jesus . . ."[1] Yes, I told myself, the devil leaves. Hold out! Hold out! They will leave! I do not see any great bravery in this. But I am happy now that I can confirm: yes, they have left!

There were two omissions that came to light just after my signing Charter 77. The first one concerned the state authorities. After seven years of service, rather unexpectedly an invitation from the district clerk, Mr Loukota, arrived for me to go to Svitavy and at a meeting of ministers sign an oath of allegiance to the Socialist Republic of Czechoslovakia. All others had signed it a long time before at the beginning of their ministry.

I arrived in Svitavy at the appointed time. On entering the conference room, I saw that the clerk was in a meeting with my Catholic colleagues. He was giving a speech which he suddenly interrupted and without an explanation asked me to come to the top table and sign the document that lay there. When I was standing on the platform I expected him to say something. But instead, he handed me a pen and showed me where to sign.

It was clear to me that he wanted to rectify the omission quickly and eradicate the long years of negligence without leaving any space for a reaction. Besides, he couldn't conceal his distaste for me. When we had dealings in private he would criticize me for being so confident that I was right. I told him once that, indeed, I tried to be right and that he could, of course, challenge me and try to prove me wrong. His reaction was impatient. It was obvious that we would never see eye to eye.

---

1 Matthew 4:11.

Now I was asked to accept like a sheep a situation which had been prepared beforehand. I had to act and therefore I said, "Mr Loukota, don't we owe the colleagues here a word of explanation?"

"And what is there to be explained, Mr Bisek?" he said.

"I'll try," I said. I was keen to seize the opportunity to make our Catholic colleagues aware of the pressure which I was experiencing. The Protestant and Catholic clergy were always kept apart by the authorities, and yet we all had to face the same hostility from the regime. I continued, "Dear colleagues, I am a minister of the Evangelical Church of Czech Brethren and my parish is in Teleci. Mr Loukota has just asked me to sign an oath of allegiance to the Socialist Republic of Czechoslovakia. I started working in my congregation seven years ago after my return from a year of studies in the USA. The regional clerk, Mr Jonas, refused to grant me a state licence for several months. Perhaps that was the reason why my oath of allegiance was forgotten."

There was some agitation in the room. I used the period of confusion to read and sign the document and then I waited to see what would happen next. Mr Loukota showed me the door and so I left. We never returned to the subject. But his resentment changed into open hostility.

By strange coincidence another similar situation happened within our church. It came to light that a group of ministers had not signed the Ministerial oath. In my case, this had also been for seven years, since the beginning of my ministry. In June 1977, I received a letter from Revd Vaclav Kejr, Synodal Senior, Moderator of the Evangelical Church of Czech Brethren. It contained a vehement admonition and request that I should no longer procrastinate about signing the Ministerial oath which I had been sent some time before, otherwise my ministry would have to be terminated. I expressed my astonishment at the harshness of the letter and remarked that I had never received any previous request. I also asked the Synodal Council to cancel the discriminatory measures by which some ministers had been asked not to attend church conferences. Until recently only ministers whose state licence had been withdrawn had not been invited. Now it was also signatories of Charter 77 who were not welcome.

In the next letter, dated 6th July 1977, I received an explanation that the reason why I had not received the original request was because of a mistake by his office. The oath to be signed was enclosed in this letter.

But I could not sign it. Having read it, I was dissatisfied, especially with the last part of the oath of allegiance which it contained. I quote: ". . . I will obey the regulations and directives of the supervising church office . . ." I saw this formulation as ambiguous because in our current situation the office supervising the church might not be part of the church but often even an enemy of the church. So I changed the wording of the last paragraph of the oath into a Christological formulation which solemnly closes a number of the church's oaths: ". . . Above all I want to seek the growth of the church in the One who is the head, that is in Jesus Christ." I sent the modified document to the Synodal Council. My knowledgeable colleagues assured me that no one would ever read the declarations and only the signatures would be checked.

The unexpected happened. The Synodal Senior read my modified oath and reacted immediately. He was indignant at my audacity. I received a summons to appear at the meeting of a special commission of the Synodal Council.

I prepared for the meeting and put together my reasons for changing the oath. I said, "Aware as I was of my humble status in the church since the beginning of my ministry, because of the daily challenges which are beyond me and which I can't comprehend, at least for my own conscience's sake I must strive not to back down but to preserve the purpose of my endeavour. I see this as possible only if I again affirm that I will give my word and my signature to the service of God alone, as at my ordination."

The commission did not reach any conclusion. And neither did they take seriously my request that they take the matter to the synod. A member of the commission told me in private that by an unfortunate coincidence the text of the oath had been drafted many years before in a time of war and it had never been duly adopted by the synod. I did not react to this; I only waited for the final resolution. It came through in a discussion with the new Synodal Senior, Revd Milan Hajek. He recommended the following compromise: Not to modify the text of the oath but to add my comments and reasons. I gratefully agreed. The final conclusion of this matter was his letter of 24th January 1978 which said that my ministerial oath had been accepted as valid by the Synodal Council. The Synodal Senior's letter ended with these words: "I hope that you will feel an inner joy at the fact that we can be in the service of our Lord, who is greater than our opinions and disagreements. May he alone straighten our path so that we will reach further understanding. Yours sincerely, Milan Hajek." It is with pleasure that I read again the conclusion of the whole affair and the words about reconciliation and understanding.

But the dealings of the Synodal Council with the ministers who sent a letter to the Federal Parliament in May 1977 had a very different outcome. The letter dealt with the relationship of the state administration to our church – the Evangelical Church of Czech Brethren. As a result of the letter the state authorities forced the leaders of the church to take disciplinary action against the signatories. We were warned and cautioned in September 1977.

Since I signed Charter 77 the State Security tried by all possible means to restrict, disturb or unsettle not only the life of our family, but also of the congregation and the church. One of the things they did was to confiscate our passports in September 1977, which had symbolic importance for us. I appealed against it immediately in a letter which said: "You justified the measures taken by quoting a section of the law without stating the specific offence committed. It is clear that there is none. A quotation of the law which is not supported by an obvious and specific offence is a blatant misuse of the law which can thus be used at any time and in any manner against anybody". We didn't receive an answer.

Another, repeated, action was a summons to the district vehicle licencing office to present our car for a technical check-up in October 1979. However we were not deprived of the vehicle licence and so prevented from using our car as so many of our friends living in towns and cities had been. That would obviously have made it much harder for the State Security to carry out surveillance comfortably. Daniela was intimidated when she was summoned to the Police Station in Policka to explain a driving offence. There she was told that she had hit another car in Policka. She just told them that she had not been aware of anything. That was enough, the policemen were satisfied.

The State Security intensified my interrogations. Sometimes they issued a summons, at other times they unexpectedly appeared in the manse saying, "So Mr Bisek, let's go" and they took me to the district town of Svitavy or, occasionally, to their regional offices in Hradec Kralove. The recurring topics were my association with anybody at any time, Charter 77 and its activities, the Church at all levels and the Church offices' disapproval of my actions, my friends who I had 'chosen badly', and the usual prompting that we should leave the country and go to 'my providers'.

I suffered greatly at that time from earache and I went to see a consultant, Dr Plachy in the town of Policka. In my case an ear examination turned out to have two parts: medical and political. It went something like this: Dr Plachy held me with his knees, put an otoscope in my ear, used it as a megaphone and in a loud whisper said, "They're after you!" I pushed him away with my elbow, eased myself from the grip of his knees, turned to him and reproachfully blurted out, "I have earache!!" Dr Plachy repeated the unusual procedure once more and I finally understood that there was something he wanted to tell me. He told me then how he had been interrogated after my last visit and how the State Security had threatened him. The result was that on my next visit I brought him the Charter 77 Document and also other materials. I had a shock on the following visit when, after the examination, Dr Plachy showed me how well he had hidden the Charter 77 materials: in the drawer of the nurse's desk! How clever! You open the drawer and there it is for everybody to see like a genie from a bottle! Poor nurse. She was as pale as ashes and did not say a thing.

I had another similar experience with a drawer, though nobody was afraid. It was at the Synodal Council, in the office of the General Secretary Mr Vales. He had been asking me to come to his office when times got hard. When I finally appeared he was angry with me for taking so long and thereby endangering not only myself but also him and the whole Church. Then he opened his drawer with the words, "Look what you're doing by not coming when I ask you to!" In the drawer were envelopes with the names of dissident ministers written on them. He handed me one with my name on it and I found some money inside. The government was trying to control the clergy by withholding salaries and Mr. Vales had been acting illegally by gathering financial support for those in trouble. It was as if he thought that the State Security were like the Syrians who were struck with blindness after Elisha's prayer in 2 Kings 6.

Personally, I did not trust the blindness of my enemies. I hid all the documents I did not want to lose in the chaff on the loft floor. Subsequently we were surprised to find out that our secret place was very near the eavesdropping device installed later by 'an unknown perpetrator'. More about that later.

The pressure intensified massively when the elders of the congregation in Teleci were interrogated in April 1978. They were told that "the minister read Charter 77 from the pulpit". The authorities knew better than those who had been present what I did during the Sunday services! All in all, the elders did not let the State Security scare them and they told the truth. Only one elder told me in tears that he hadn't protested against some of the false accusations. I tried to reassure him and I told him that lies and a hostile authority must not separate us. Before God we both knew how things were. We avoided being separated, but I sensed that we could receive the last solace only from the One who keeps the course of all things in his hand.

The regime did not give up the idea that it might be possible to separate me from the community in Teleci and so ultimately to stop my influence. Therefore the regional government clerk, Mr Kamenik, asked the Moderator of the Presbytery, Mr Vyborny, to call a meeting of the elders in Teleci in the manse on the 10th of December 1980. The district government clerk, Mr Loukota, was to be present as well. When I think of it now, I can still hardly believe it: The Moderator complied with them and I received a notification from him saying, ". . . Your presence and the presence of all the elders is required. I am looking forward to meeting you. With brotherly regards, Jindrich Vyborny, Moderator."

At the meeting, the regional government clerk read a list of ten irrefutable examples of my anti-state activities. All of them concerned my opinions and conduct because I was 'a public figure' and therefore I was expected to conform with regard to the issue of the Warsaw Pact brotherly military assistance in 1968, to vote in elections and to agree with public pronouncements. My stance was anti-State and my contacts with other dissidents were the evidence. He supported this last point with an example, saying, "I wouldn't have expected to see Mr Bisek in Hradec Kralove in connection with the trial of the leading dissident Jaroslav Sabata. Mr Bisek travels wherever he wants. Indeed!" And he finished off by saying, "We don't want to be chopping off heads, but Mr Bisek has been doing all this for ten years already!" The district clerk added his comment about 'the arrogance' with which I always presented myself.

The last to speak was the Moderator. He told us about the state authorities' forbearance, that the signatories of Charter 77 in the Presbytery were not small children and how grateful we were that there had been no hard-line sanctions as yet. Was he trying to prevent the worst from happening? After a longer silence all eyes rested on me. But I simply wasn't ready to speak immediately after their high-handed performances. In the end, the Moderator asked the regional clerk if I was allowed to speak. He said, "That's what we're waiting for".

In my reply I rejected all the criticism and said that it was evident that my rights to freedom of opinion and movement were being curtailed. I said a few words about the Helsinki Agreement of 1976 and the hope it had inspired. After a while some of the elders spoke in a positive way about my work in the congregation. Antonin Lamplot said, "Mr Bisek has put his head in a noose. If he hadn't wanted to fight he could have thrown in the towel. I couldn't criticise him . . ." The organist, Boda Filipi, said that as he saw it, the elders had been summoned to force Mr Bisek to leave the congregation. He also mentioned how parents from Teleci had been summoned to the local council and warned against enrolling their children in religious classes. The session clerk, Josef Dvorak, spoke about my interpretation of the gospel, about my idealism and Dr Martin Luther King. Marta Dankova remembered how the children who wanted to attend the bible class had to sneak secretly into the manse. Then she asked what the outcome of the meeting was supposed to be. The regional clerk said that every minister had taken an oath of allegiance to the Czechoslovak Socialist State and that they were ready to continue in dialogue with Mr Bisek. He added that they were expecting to receive the elders' response in writing by the end of the year.

The elders duly sent this letter off on 15th December 1980:

> The elders of the Evangelical Church of Czech Brethren in Teleci express their opinion of the activities of the Reverend Tomas Bisek.
>
> Mr Bisek has always fulfilled all the responsibilities that his job entails. He conducts Sunday services regularly not only in Teleci but also in Breziny. He teaches religious classes regularly. He conducts all the funeral ceremonies that he is asked to do in a dignified manner. He visits the sick members of the congregation.
>
> We also value the way Mr Bisek and his wife have attended to the recent repairs on the church building. Mr

Bisek found skilled workers and helpers who put up scaf-
folding so that the outer coating could be renewed. Then he
found workers who would paint the top of the spire of the
church. His help was considerable in all these manual tasks.
His wife cooked for the workers for the whole duration of
the repairs. They both contributed to the completion of the
repairs through their exemplary and dedicated work. This
year, the church organ was repaired and again it was done
through Mr Bisek's endeavours.

The conduct of Mr Bisek as a citizen has its basis in his
deepest Christian convictions, his faith and conscience. Mr
Bisek is an honest citizen, who fulfils his responsibilities.
He is very diligent. He cares for his family in a responsible
way. He is willing to help with all that is for the good of
society.

We declare that Mr Bisek has done nothing that would
contradict the Constitution of this country.

Signed . . .

Reading through all this again I see how, after the aggressive speeches
of the government officials and my refusal to accept them, there was
a sense of freedom at the meeting and it appeared also in the elders'
letter. Where had the fear and worry gone? How come that after
massive threats people could feel free? Does it not show that the spirit
can't be imprisoned?

The government officials, fully protected and authorized to
start a very carefully prepared campaign, did not understand the
situation. Most of the elders were carrying within them wounds from
the past caused by enforced collectivisation. They felt uprooted and
in many ways lost in the world in which they lived. And now, two
representatives of a power which violated their rights had come to
their manse. Was there nowhere to hide, nowhere to turn to? Then
the Word about God's sovereignty and might, about Christ's sacrifice
and his victory over the last enemy, was heard on the congregation's
own ground. At the moment of confrontation with an alien power I
could not deny my rights. I had no choice. I would have denied what I
preached. I would have denied what I had anxiously and fearfully put
my signature to and what I guaranteed with my life. I was pronounced
the enemy of the regime and 'evidence' was produced. Was it really

evidence? All the false and fabricated arguments had been presented as reality.

And there I was, led to express my protest in full by the One God who had called me to his service. It was not my doing that there was light in the darkness. Those who I had been meeting before the face of God on Sundays and weekdays for ten years were not able or willing to deny me. In our Teleci manse we were granted what the church was denied. The Evangelical Church of Czech Brethren allowed the authorities to tear it to pieces. In the Teleci manse, there were moments given by God, the One who always knew what to do and did it for us: God split the darkness and chased it away!

Of course, normal days returned and life was not easy for us for the next five years, until we left for Scotland. But what we had a foretaste of has stayed with us. What did I learn?

First of all, I know that not I, but the Spirit of the Lord, bestows the gift of freedom. I also know that at times of confrontation it is not possible to go half-way and manoeuvre, cover up, and hope for reconciliation, peace and the reign of enlightenment. That would be only what Havel calls 'self-motion' and a debased and unproductive way of life. Only when finally a bright light of understanding, truth and justice shines, can we hope that brothers and sisters will embrace one another – and be of one spirit.

Chapter 9

FRIENDS

There are some of our friends I would like to mention, because they were the closest and most faithful at that time – first, the neighbouring ministers who signed Charter 77 – Pavel Hlavac, Jan Keller and Bohdan Pivonka.

Pavel and I went to Prague together to sign the document. It was in the flat of the philosopher Ladislav Hejdanek. We were talking and, at the same time, we signed our statement written on a small piece of paper. It went something like this: "I, Tomas Bisek, agree with the Charter 77 Document and add my signature." The statement was dated. Then we drove back to the Uplands as fast as we could. Would Prague disappear into a black hole and take us with it? No, it would not. There was no earthquake, no tanks from left or right, nor an end of the world. Daniela was unhappy when I got home. She had asked me to add her signature too, but I was not able to overcome my anxiety. Not long afterwards she did manage to write her statement and sign it.

I also remember Pavel standing up at an annual Presbytery meeting and saying boldly, "I simply do not wish my children to be educated in a communist school." A government official was sitting at the back. On another occasion Pavel told us how pleasing it was to be at a church meeting where there was an atmosphere of openness, trust and confidentiality. It would not have been me if I did not chip in, "Don't you know, Pavel, that where two or three are gathered together, one of them is an informer?" Pavel could not take it at all. "I'll punch you!" he said. Now he knows, and we all know, that I was right – or maybe not.

Jan Keller coped with the period of Charter 77 in a peculiar way. In contrast to his talkative colleagues he managed not to speak at interrogations and so the time he had to spend with the State Security was relatively short. By the Moderator, however, and also by some members of the session in his church he was sometimes chastised like a young boy. Was it because he was so open and had a particular order of priorities? The authorities made him leave the parish in our area and, shortly after settling in a new congregation, his licence was revoked. "Unreported summer activities with young people and children" brought him to court and unfounded allegations of paedophilia were also filed, although unsuccessfully. The solidarity of colleagues, the leadership of the whole church and signatories of Charter 77 prevented the worst, which would have been a conviction. After the Velvet Revolution in 1990, he became the mayor of the small town in our area where he had been the minister in the seventies. The prerequisite was, however, that he be made a citizen of the town, because his permanent residence was somewhere else. Jan was the mayor for two consecutive terms.

I remember Bohdan Pivonka first with a letter to his congregation in which he commended the members to the protection of the right hand of the Lord (as in Psalm 63). The authorities saw the word 'right' as a provocation. Then I see Bohdan on his small moped, arriving intentionally straight into the hands of the police, who were besieging our manse for three days at the time of the big trial with Vaclav Havel and others in Prague in October 1979. I was under overt surveillance, in order to be prevented from attending the hearing. My next memory of Bohdan is when he took away the bugging system I had found in our manse, for he had offered to arrange for a detailed analysis of the device. A few weeks passed and Bohdan and I were taken by the criminal police to the regional Prosecutor to hand the device over officially. Bohdan was my witness.

We lived through all kinds of uncertainties together with all these people. However, we also kept finding remarkable assurance and pleasure at discovering similarities in our views and mutual understanding.

In the tense moments, when the State Security intensified their interest in me, Jan and Milena Simsa were among those who tried to be very helpful and caring. I see Jan at the wedding of a dissident couple in Teleci. The reception was in the manse garden and I hear Jan advise the groom: "The husband should always listen carefully to his wife. For example, she asks, have you put a film in your camera?" (There were no digital cameras then.) Shortly afterwards Jan discovered that he had been taking a lot of pictures with no film.

The Simsas also invited our two boys to visit them in Brno on several occasions. They always carefully prepared a very full programme for them. Lukas and Benjamin would return home totally exhausted. We were grateful to Jan and Milena for introducing us to their friend, a philosopher, Bozena Komarkova, also a signatory of Charter 77. Later, when I came to her for advice, she very wisely advised me to discuss my finding of a bugging system in our manse with Dr Jiri Hajek, a signatory of Charter 77 and a former Minister of Foreign Affairs in the Dubcek Cabinet, so that he could tell me what steps to take in order that the State Security could not cover it up.

Jan's licence was also revoked and he had to leave the village of Prosetin. Bozena Komarkova commented on the stance of the Prosetin congregation, "They just go on living their private lives . . ."

When our friends were trying to think of ways to keep us in the country, Milena remarked of our preparations to emigrate, "Those who speak about their plans to leave have already decided to go. There's no use trying to stop them." This was not a general statement. It was an existential description of the state of mind of those who stop thinking in a rational way. They are, in fact, on the way already . . .

I remember the words of two outstanding friends and mentors of ours. This is how I understood them: Bozena Komarkova said, "You don't get rid of your problems by going somewhere else. They'll just be different". Freda Kocab said something similar, "Why should I leave? I'll still be carrying my burden anyway".

Our close friendship with Vera and Pavel Roubal was remarkable for us. We were driving through a foggy night to Kytlice, a small settlement in the north-west of Bohemia. We arrived in the small hours and Pavel was not in. He had had to go to the forest and make sure that the remains of the bonfires where he burnt branches and twigs during the day would not cause a fire. Both Vera and Pavel were graduates of the Technical University. As their youngest, Petr, suffered from severe asthma, they could not live in Prague. From Kytlice they soon moved to the south of Bohemia and Pavel exchanged forestry work for a job in a factory where they made brushes. Once he refused to make a donation in aid of Vietnam. His shop floor manager put in the token amount of ten Crowns for Pavel. This upset Pavel and he said, "How can I be sure that the ten Crowns won't support armaments in Vietnam?" The manager did not understand and found it unreasonable to have to strike Pavel off the list of donors. He would be the only one missing. Was Pavel's standpoint absurd? It was certainly futile, in the sense that Czechoslovakia had been selling and giving arms to many countries for a long time. It was 'normal' – or should we not accept that?

In our manse in Teleci Pavel got acquainted with the writings of Professor Josef B. Soucek. He read Soucek's biblical commentaries with respect. I remember Pavel also for his regular presence at court hearings where he went in support of the Chartists and other unjustly tried people. For us, the supporters, it meant standing outside the court building and being identified and checked by the State Security. Sometimes an interrogation followed. At the time of the Velvet Revolution, Pavel initiated the founding of several Civic Forum[1] Groups in the area where he lived. It led to his total exhaustion and, after a long illness, he died at work, taking his own life . . .

Vera was left alone with four children. They did not stay in South Bohemia, but moved to Prague. Vera began her tireless work with asylum seekers, mainly from the east and, at the time of the Balkan Wars, also from the south. There is one more thing I like to remember about Vera and Pavel Roubal whenever we go swimming in the open air. They would say, "No, we don't have a towel. You don't need one if you get dressed immediately. You'll feel warm, you see?"

In our extended family we saw the impressive leaning of Vera and Pavel Sadilek towards us, the Chartists. Pavel was Daniela's eldest cousin. When contacts with the Chartists were dangerous, he would never renounce his relatives. Once we told them that the Roubal family had settled in the area. The Sadileks took it as an invitation to make friends with them. The friendship has lasted almost twenty years so far. The Sadileks must have known that contacts with active supporters of human rights might be dangerous. However, they gradually and openly started to support Chartists and those who were in danger.

To his new political orientation, Pavel Sadilek later also added a return to the family tradition of membership in the Evangelical Church of Czech Brethren. He became an elder in the small preaching station in Kamenice and Lipou. All this happened after the fall of the old regime, when he was elected mayor of the town. He accepted with great responsibility the role of the one who had to deal democratically

---

1 Civic Forum was a political movement in the Czech part of Czechoslovakia, established during the Velvet Revolution in 1989.

with everybody, even those who had opposed the change. He would say hello to neighbours whom he did not have to see and did not even like before. It is encouraging to see how people do not have to change quickly and at a fixed moment, but the change can happen in small, sometimes hardly perceptible steps. These gradual steps, when viewed as a whole, constitute my vision of how the orientation of a life can change, much better than a sudden revelation or a passionate about-turn which may claim to be complete and perfect. Perfection in five minutes. Real perfection in five minutes?

Among our nearest and dearest we found steadfast support, for example even in the most dramatic moments, in Lydie, Daniela's sister, and her husband Pavel. They had had the idea that our eldest, Lucie, could live with them, in the anonymity of Prague, in her last year of primary school, so that she would have a better chance of being accepted into a grammar school. It paid off. A transfer to the grammar school in Policka near Teleci was not a problem after she had been accepted in Prague. Lydie and Pavel never changed the regularity of their visits to us even when the atmosphere became rather tense because of the authorities' interest in us. I can still see Lydie, in tears, helping us to prepare for moving to Scotland. Our relationship has been changing, but it is a lasting one. We managed to get together before the change in 1989 in Switzerland and they saw us a few times in Scotland. Today, we meet regularly in Prague.

However, we also saw how relationships in the closest family were affected by the disrupting pressure of repression, called 'salami policy'. 'Slicing the salami' meant depriving activists of their supportive friends, one by one, so that they would be weakened and isolated. I noticed it when at almost every interrogation I would hear, "Get rid of the friends who make your life difficult".

"What do you mean?" I would ask.

Their reply was clear, "You know perfectly well." So they wanted me to apply self-censorship! I asked them if I should be choosing my friends depending on whether I would consider them an asset. Their response was unambiguous, "Of course!"

"And you make friends like that?" I asked and they replied, "Of course we do. How else?"

A special friendship developed from a spontaneous visit by Anna Sabatova and Petr Uhl with their toddler son and baby girl to our manse in Teleci one morning at seven o'clock. It sounds very unusual, but it was an arranged visit. I saw Petr first at an informal meeting of Chartists in Prague and he accepted my invitation for their family to visit us. After the first visit they came to Teleci regularly for several years.

Being with the Uhls meant an endless conversation. My ministerial and pastoral duties were constantly being disrupted by my having to retype issues of 'Information about the Charter' in thirteen copies. We were also passionate night-time players of Scrabble in Czech. In Teleci, Anna and Petr found respite from the never ending surveillance in Prague. For a period, there was even a policeman sitting in front of their door on the third floor in Anglicka Street in the centre of Prague at all times. I remember going to see them, taking a bag of potatoes from our village to have a reason for my visit. I was stopped and my identity documents were checked. I was told I had no business seeing the Uhls. At that very moment, somebody from inside the flat opened the door and a firm hand grabbed me and pulled me in. The potatoes were 'duly delivered'. How I got out into the street again, I no longer remember . . .

The Uhls' visits also meant an expansion of our family. Our four children were joined by Pavel and Sasa. Pavel was always trying to secure his rightful place in the boys' gang. Being the youngest, it was a constant struggle for him. He was always looking for our boys and the question he always asked, worded and pronounced very carefully, still rings in my ears, "Tomas, can you tell me where they are?" Our boys liked and accepted Pavel, but his age prevented him from doing everything with them in the vast space of the countryside.

Sasa was a contented baby and I did not notice her much. I only know that we all soon became one family, which was confirmed during Petr's imprisonment in a high security prison for five and a half years. With a lump in my throat I still see the preparations for visiting Petr scheduled for once every six months. Daniela, Anna and her children would leave early on a Sunday morning and I, in two minds, would lead the Sunday service. They would return in the afternoon, Anna in a pitiful state because of the hostile and cruel atmosphere in the prison during their visit. Her depression used to last several days. At times, she was threatened that she too would end up in prison . . . I remember a dream that Anna had when her husband was in prison and she was alone with her children. In her dream she was standing on her bed swinging a long cudgel around, so that the State Security could not get at her. I rejoice that they never did.

Chapter 10

BUGS!

Contacts with Chartists like Anna Sabatova, Petr Uhl and their children resulted for us in a more intensive interest by the State Security in the manse in Teleci. Gradually, as if suspicion crept in from outside, we began to hesitate when we wanted to mention arrangements to meet somebody or discuss a planned visit or what would happen in the next few days. These premonitions were strengthened by the wise comments of Daniela's mother, who thought it was necessary that we keep all Charter texts in a safe place and cover the telephone receiver when we wanted to share political jokes. She saw it as a symbolic ear belonging to a police informer. She was right, as we later discovered. Only the technical details were more sophisticated . . .

Our uneasiness grew, especially during the period in 1979 when we had the most visitors in the manse. Then, suddenly, an unexpected piece of information and a warning came and confirmed our anxiety. One day at the post office the post master and I had an unusual conversation. He was a member of the Communist Party and had spoken to me perhaps only once before. The first conversation was no less unusual than the second. The first time, he asked me which newspaper I subscribed to, explaining that he had to fill in a form about me. I refused to help him and told him that, as he knew, I only got our church paper. He suggested adding the 'Literary Papers' to improve my profile. He was confused as to why I did not agree to that, for, as everybody knew, that was the way it should be done.

The next conversation developed like this: I was standing at the post office counter and, as usual, expected to be given a pack of letters through the small opening. Instead, the post master leant forward and blurted out, "Your house is being bugged".

I reacted sharply, "Did you say something?"

He replied immediately, "No".

I said, "So, go on".

The post master continued, and even now I can hardly believe it: "Strange men keep coming to the house opposite the shop and they seem to be doing something. Perhaps someone wants to know what you talk about at home."

I did not ask any more. I just wanted to know exactly which house it was and who lived there. The upper floor had been empty for some time, I was told. The conversation ended with me saying, "Thank you for not telling me anything." The post master said, "You're welcome," and handed me my letters.

Back at home, Daniela and I thought hard what to do next. It was clear to us that we must weigh very carefully what we could say at home and when we should leave the house to talk. We both also felt that we should find out what it was all about.

First of all, we walked to the house the postmaster had mentioned, which was about half a mile away. We saw that there was a new telephone line leading from the first floor across the road to a telephone post at the Vondrak shop. What about the routine of life on the first floor? Would it match our routine in the manse, which was different from the rhythm of the village? We decided to go as if to bed and then walk back to the house to see if anything was happening there. And so, late at night, in pitch darkness, we walked to a place from where we could see the house and the light in the windows on the first floor. After a while the lights went out and the car parked in front of the house left. There was silence. We didn't have the slightest doubt that the activity there concerned us. It was a very peculiar feeling. We thought of the many guests who had visited us during the period concerned, many of them from Charter 77 circles. What did we talk about with our visitors? Our guests discussed things freely believing that one could talk about anything in the manse in a small village! The Synodal Senior had visited the congregation and we had a very vocal confrontation about the meaning of Charter 77, about truth as the heritage of John Hus, and also about the meaning of the work of the church and its ministers. A great number of Chartists from Brno and Prague had gathered on the occasion of the marriage of Brona and Jiri Muller. And there had been many others from Charter 77, from the church and our family. We understood the tactics of the State Security: in a remote place like our manse in the Bohemian Uplands, they could get the most important information: information with a capital I.

"How can we live? What about our four children? How will this end? Is there a way of protecting ourselves?" we kept asking ourselves. It was like the situation a close colleague and friend, Bohdan Pivonka, had gone through during the Stalinist era in the fifties. His parents were active members of the Salvation Army in Prague. Thanks to his curiosity, young Bohdan found an eavesdropping device in the attic exactly above their flat. He immediately told his parents about it. Such a thing was life threatening at the time. After that his parents almost always spoke outside and in due time the device 'disappeared'. For the family it was a miraculous and narrow escape.

Should we be acting in a similar way? We tried to. But then an almost unbelievable sequence of events started to unfold. I can easily put a date to it, because it was at the time of the biggest trial of Charter 77 signatories called 'Petr Uhl and others'. It was the end of October 1979. We knew some of the other people who were to be tried with Petr Uhl, for example Vaclav Havel, Otka Bednarova, Vaclav Maly, Dana Nemcova and others. I learned directly from my State Security guardians when the trial would begin. It was a Friday when a State Security car stopped in front of the manse. The State Security men gave me a very plain warning: "Mr Bisek, if you move in the direction of Prague this Monday, you'll be detained." Then, on Sunday, I was resting in the living room after the service. In the short period of peace and quiet I looked up at the ceiling. A small speck in the white-washed surface caught my eye. There were countless similar ones. Today I know that, actually, I saw a needle in a haystack. I climbed on a chair and poked the spot with a fingernail. The whitewash fell off and I saw a metal ring of about one third of an inch in diameter.

I could not help assuming what it might be. I fetched a stepladder and measured the position of the ring. I went to the attic, measured the distance from the wall and lifted some planks that lay there. Then I groped around in the chaff that filled the space between the ceiling and the attic floor. I stuck my arm into the chaff up to my shoulder and felt something hard on my elbow. It was a black box. I took it out and put it to my ear. I heard a buzzing sound. I assumed it was electric current and I disconnected it. The box went silent.

My head was spinning. I ran downstairs and told Daniela that a war had started. We both understood that we were in a dangerous situation. I ran back to the attic and continued to look for more. I found two wires leading from the now silent box. They ran into the chaff. The shorter one led me to my 'ring' in the living room. The ring was, in fact, a tube which came out of a small cube, smaller than a cube of sugar. On it were traces of something similar to plasticine, so that the microphone could easily be pulled out in a hurry. The other wire led towards the kitchen. I pulled at it and soon I held another microphone in my hand. The length of the wire suggested that it had 'listened' to what was said in the kitchen. I never found the exact location in the kitchen ceiling.

Daniela and I tried to imagine how the device could have got there, but there was no time to discuss it. I wanted to find out as much as I could immediately, because I was so worried that they might come to get it. I discovered that the black box, an amplifier, was connected to our telephone line. Someone had had to drill through a stone wall, one and a half meters in all, from the attic to the corner of a doorway. There the wire joined our telephone line. It was not difficult to find it as the perpetrator was rather careless and left a big splinter that had fallen off just loosely attached. He must have thought it unlikely that anyone would find this connection hidden in the lintel of the door. It was clear that this action had been planned in great detail and specialised equipment had had to be used to carry it out.

I didn't manage to discover any more at that moment. I couldn't cancel the afternoon service at the preaching station of Breziny. And I still did not know where the amplifier was connected to the electric circuit. In spite of this my colleague and friend Bohdan took away the device that very day and passed it on so that we could get an expert opinion. We did not know and therefore could not tell where it had been taken. We felt relieved that the first wave of anxiety that the manse would be raided and the device would disappear had gone. If it had been taken away, it would intensify our helplessness if we attempted to testify to 'something that did not exist', as the State Security would claim.

The next day, on Monday, the trial in Prague began. It was also a day when my Presbytery had their monthly meeting, this time in the manse in Krucemburk. Daniela and I found it very difficult to get any sleep and kept whispering and reassuring ourselves that we had done all we could and all that was necessary. We also considered what to do next.

At about six in the morning on the Monday, I looked out and saw a police Volha car parked in the driveway. The manse was under police surveillance. I got ready for my Presbytery meeting and left the house. A policeman jumped out of the car and asked, "Where are you going, Mr Bisek?" I said, "To a meeting in Krucemburk". He said, "We're coming with you". They let me take my car out and then followed me. When we got back in the afternoon, I put the car back in the garage and they blocked the driveway again. They continued to patrol the manse.

Daniela and the children had unusual visitors during my absence. First, there was a knock at the kitchen door. To Daniela's question, "Who's that?" came an unusual answer, "Don't be afraid, Mrs Bisek." These could be words from God, or a sly false reassurance from the devil. "We're coming from the regional fire brigade!" When Daniela told me how the three men introduced themselves, both of us knew who they were: that was the way in which visitors from the plain clothes police introduced themselves. They had clearly come to have a look at what had happened to their device. My absence made it easier for them. Their way of checking if the house was all right as far as fire safety was concerned consisted of looking at our ceilings. Then they went upstairs to the attic. They looked around and asked if the children played there. Finally, they left without any other comment, criticism or recommendation.

My further investigation of the attic space confirmed why they were so interested in whether children played there: the connection to the 220V circuit lay bare in a far corner of the attic, above the church hall. The danger that fire might consume the whole house and the family did not concern them. They only wanted to be sure that the children had not disconnected it while playing. The 'fire commission' looked for the simplest explanation for the microphones not working. I visibly disturbed the wiring only after their visit. The observant visitors did not find out why the system was inactive. But we had to reckon that they would repeat their visit. Would they wait until we were out? At that moment we remembered how we had returned from a visit to Prague one evening last spring and wondered that we had not locked any of the doors and the door to the yard had been left ajar. Had somebody left in a hurry? Now the question turned into a certainty.

We also remembered how our organist, Boda, had admonished us that when we left for a couple of days we didn't lock up. We tried to improve. Once we had just got back and Boda came to see us and said,

"You're getting better. I found the place locked up. But the key was left in the front door!"

Later here was another follow up to the visit of the 'regional fire safety commission'. After the Velvet Revolution I met my forestry mate, Mirek. He used to be a member of the volunteer fire brigade in Teleci. We spent three years in the forest as workmates and friends. He never asked me about the bugs. But now, after the Velvet Revolution, it was one of his first questions: "Tomas, can you tell me, who were the two other men who came to check the fire safety of the manse? I knew the one who was from the regional fire safety commission but I had never met the other two." I replied, "Yes, I can tell you that they were State Security men, secret policemen." Now Mirek understood why I had been so upset when he and his colleagues from the local fire brigade came to check the fire safety in the manse. I asked them to leave because it was only a few days since the visit from the region. I told them: "Your colleagues from the region have just been here! So what do you want?" They did not understand at all and they did not dare to ask what had happened.

A peculiar calm followed the visit of the regional fire safety brigade. It was tense with our apprehension as to whether they would come before we could get advice on how we should proceed. We needed to get technical expertise and we also wanted to have a clearer idea about the legal aspect of the matter. We had to get in touch with those who knew the answers. But it was necessary not to leave the manse empty, so that uninvited guests would not be tempted to enter. It meant that someone had to be in at all times. And so Daniela would take the car from the garage and drive to the train station 'all alone' with me hidden under a blanket on the floor behind the seats. I got to Brno like this to see Professor Komarkova. On her advice, several days later, I also travelled to Prague to see the philosopher Ladislav Hejdanek, who took me to see Professor Jiri Hajek.

Yes, I learned that in a country ruled by the Communist Party and directed from the Soviet Union there was no independent prosecutor. The closest similar role would be that of the general or regional procurator. A 'just social order' did not need anything else. The idea that the device could secretly be transported abroad to get an independent assessment was no good. Comrades would just laugh at that. Of course, everybody knew how deceitful capitalists were.

Bohdan Pivonka was able to secure technical expertise about the device and so everything was ready for me to inform the state procurator. But, at this point, the State Security managed to intervene. It was really at the last moment, in a way similar to the chase in Prague back in January 1977 when the representatives of Charter 77 were taking a document with the names of the first signatories to the Castle; that is to the President's office. We too were caught 'red-handed'.

It was three weeks after my discovery of the device when, one evening, the manse was suddenly surrounded by several police cars and a number of State Security officers entered the house. They forcefully demanded that they be given "the device, Mr Bisek, which you have been spreading alarming news about and so slandering the State Security". To my question as to what it was all about they said, "The Biseks are telling their friends in Charter 77 and in the church that the State Security have installed an eavesdropping device in the Teleci manse". I told them that I had really found something which, in my opinion, was a listening device and I was going to send a letter to the general procurator and file a complaint against an unknown perpetrator. 'OK, give us the device and we'll take care of it,' they said. I said that I could not.

"Why?" they asked. "What are your reasons?" I said, "I can't be sure that you would not say that I mistook a toothbrush for an eavesdropping device." "Mr Bisek," they said, "you are asking us to turn your house inside out!" I said, "I can't, of course, prevent you from doing that." And so it went on and on. They wanted to know who I had told about it. They learned that I had told anybody who asked me about it. They concluded that we had spoken about it everywhere. In the end, they did not search the manse, probably because I told them that it would be necessary to search in a much larger area. But their questions changed into threats: "You'll end up in jail for longer than the five years that your friend Petr Uhl is serving. This attitude of yours will break your neck."

They assumed I was aware that their new methods meant they could control and intimidate me without physical brutality. When I kept repeating that I would give the device only to the general procurator they told me to say good-bye to my wife, who I would not be seeing for some time. They were not willing to leave us on our own and so I just pushed them out of the door. I had only a very short moment with Daniela and we agreed that Bohdan needed to know that we had to get the device back. It was a task for Daniela. The State Security men were with us within a minute and without a word or further delay they took me to the familiar police interrogation room in Svitavy.

There our negotiations continued in the form of an interrogation. The recurring theme was where and when I would hand the device over to them. I persisted in saying that I would give it only to the general procurator. It was already past midnight and I saw that the interrogators were tired. It seemed to me that not even taking turns helped them very much. At one point another State Security man entered and without any introduction interrupted the questioning and said, "Mr Bisek, we haven't been able to contact the general procurator. Do you still insist on seeing him?" I indicated that it was not my problem and the State Security man left without a word. A peculiar time of quiet without any questions followed. The night went by at an even slower pace than before. I yearned for some support. I contemplated whether I could perhaps take my Bible out of my pocket and read a few verses from the Psalms and a few words from the gospels. I felt the warmth of the small book but I was afraid to take it out because my interrogators might grab it and take it from me. If I lost it . . .

During another long spell of quiet I felt more encouraged and found myself holding my New Testament. I opened it and I heard, "What are you reading, Mr Bisek?" I did not answer immediately. I tried to understand the real meaning of the question. And the State Security man continued, "Is this that Bible of yours?" And then I answered, "No, it's only the second part. The one that tells about Jesus Christ." The State Security man continued in a surprising way, "Is he the one who was friendly with thieves and women from the street?" "Yes, it's him," I answered. And he continued, "And he would invite us to his table too, wouldn't he?" I could not believe my ears and blurted out, "Yes! . . . But there is, in fact, one condition. You would have to want it." There were no more questions. But I could not read. I put my New Testament back in my pocket knowing that what had just happened was giving witness and it would not happen again. I am still in awe of it.

But it was not yet the end of the night's interrogation. What followed was mostly silence. I understood that my interrogators were waiting for instructions. Then the State Security man who had appeared before to tell me about the general procurator came in again with the same information – the general procurator could not be reached. Would I accept a regional procurator instead? He was ready to see me in the morning. I agreed but gave them my conditions. I knew I would have to have the device with me and I insisted on two witnesses coming along. One would be Bohdan Pivonka, who had been the interim Moderator in Teleci, and the other would be our Moderator in the Presbytery. Then I was taken back home. The manse was still under heavy surveillance.

There was no time to rejoice at my return. It wasn't only because of all the tension, but also because of the very difficult task Daniela was required to carry out: to get the device from Bohdan, who lived in Svratouch, twenty kilometres from Teleci. How would she get away from the manse? How would she get to Svratouch? Would she get back in time?

It was still dark when she left through the bedroom window at the back of the house and climbed over the wall to a field, ran along the cemetery wall and down the slope to the bus stop. What she did not know was that somebody had erected a wire fence across one of the fields. By the time she got round it, the bus she had to catch had gone. The hope that somebody in the village might be up and willing to take her to Svratouch helped her to keep going and walk up through the village. There was a light in the window of our organist, Boda, who lived at the top end. Boda did not ask any questions, got into his Skoda car and drove Daniela to the Svratouch manse, where Daniela fetched a bag, and Boda drove her back again. She had to ask him not to go too near the manse in Teleci because she had to get back unnoticed. The mission was accomplished in good time and we were ready for the police. To this day we admire Boda, the most talkative person in the congregation, who helped without ever asking what it was all about.

At 8 am the doorbell rang. I opened the front door only as much as the safety chain allowed me. There was a polite voice outside saying, "Good morning, sir, I am from the criminal investigation department. We are supposed to take you to Hradec Kralove to a regional procurator." He handed me his badge through the narrow opening of the door. I copied his number and opened the door for him to enter. I got ready to go. When I was outside the front of the manse, I stopped and said as firmly as I could that I would not go anywhere until the children were allowed to go to school. The CID officer spoke to the policemen who were patrolling the manse making sure that no one went either in or out, and came back with the words, "Your children can go to school". I went back home to get the children. Then I waited until I saw that a policeman accompanied them to school. Then the CID officer and I got into the waiting car. But the driver did not yet get the order to go. Instead, the CID officer explained in great detail what would happen: I would hold 'the thing' at all times, he would watch me all the time, so that I could not give anything to anybody nor accept anything from anybody.

Then we drove to Svratouch, where Bohdan joined us. But in Rana, the place where our Moderator lived, we heard that he was at a meeting of ministers with the district secretary in Chrudim. I still insisted on the Moderator's presence and so we had to get him. When we reached the district offices in Chrudim, the CID officer and I went in to collect the Moderator. When the CID officer called the district secretary out of the meeting room, I shouted over his shoulder, "It's because of an eavesdropping device!" I could see how everybody in the room was stunned.

The journey continued with the CID officer constantly checking the three of us in the back seat, so that we would not pass anything between us. When we arrived in Hradec Kralove and stopped in front of the regional offices, the CID officer jumped out of the car and disappeared to look for a regional Procurator. After a while we asked the driver if he was in charge of us. He said, "No, I'm only the driver". So we got out of the car to stretch our legs. The driver did not react. After some time, the officer returned and took us to the Procurator. But I was invited in alone with the explanation that my witnesses should wait until the report had been written. The Procurator's secretary was asked to leave and the Procurator found typing rather arduous. I dictated to him the text of the expert opinion I had brought with me and asked him, "Why doesn't the secretary do the typing?" He replied, "Economizing". But I thought that the reason was in fact so that as few people as possible would know about it. At the end of the procedure the Procurator was surprised when I remarked that there were two witnesses waiting outside the door. "I had completely forgotten!" he said. I recognized this type of 'forgetfulness'. When my witnesses had been called in, I showed them the device, which Bohdan was familiar with, and all of us signed the report.

Did this war of ours end then? No, not yet. Several months later a regional Procurator for special affairs summoned Daniela to the Police Station in Policka where he questioned her. Then he came to see the manse. He took photographs of the site where I had found the device. Seeing it he did not hide his indignation at the way the device had been installed and said, "There must have been a special work party here. Can you explain it?" Then he apologised. He said it was the first time he had seen such a thing and he had not realised that we could not know the answer.

I was also summoned to Hradec Kralove again for more questioning. After a few months a judicial report arrived. It said: ". . . The device consisted of some parts which could have been used at the time of the Second World War, and parts that were new. Expert opinion suggests that this device could be used to record conversations held in the above-mentioned building. It cannot be stated whether listening to the Bisek family and their guests was the reason for the installation of the device, nor if its installation and subsequent discovery should compromise the Czechoslovak State Police. For these reasons the court case against an unknown perpetrator has been closed."

This was a full stop after our resolute battle with the repressive system. Friends who had some experience with situations similar to ours said that we had managed to make our case successfully. They also said that we should expect retaliation. The pattern of the work of the State Security suggested that this might take about three years, during which the victim would be followed, so that all contacts could be recorded. Did that mean three more years of uncertainty? What then could be counted as a victory and what was actually a defeat in a totalitarian system?

Chapter 11

THE STRUGGLE CONTINUES

However, our case demonstrated the slackening of the original revolutionary zeal. It seemed that uncertainties had crept in and affected the state's methods of enforcing its power. Otherwise, why would they have brute force crushing us for years and then employ a multitude of instruments of state power to make a rural minister from a tiny village in the Bohemian Uplands hand over an eavesdropping device about which a state authority said that it was most probably the minister himself who had installed it? What were the authorities afraid of? They persisted in their case and verbally assured themselves of their total dominance. Wasn't it fear that was a very dangerous and unpredictable motivation for their actions?

How were we to overcome our anxiety? What could uphold us in the following days and months? The solidarity between Daniela and me was sure and certain. It clearly carried us through the direct confrontation with the power of the state. We were able to share our impressions only when that peculiar time began to return to normal. We rejoiced that we were still together and we felt closer to one another. The support of many people from Charter 77 circles was tangible. Colleagues from the nearest manses were able to appear unexpectedly even though it was clear that they would be checked and warned off by the police. We were also aware of the sympathy towards us shown by some neighbours and members of the congregation.

To demonstrate the sheer kindness shown to us, we like to remember Mrs Smatlanova from the local group of Catholics. More than once she climbed the slope up to the manse in darkness which felt even darker in the general atmosphere of fear at what sanctions might be used. She would go round the house to the back door, hand us a bowl of strawberries, and quickly disappear into the darkness. There was also our neighbour, old Mr Teply. He lived beside the road below the manse. The roof of his house tempted our children to throw stones down on it. He only occasionally complained about it. Once, when, he met Daniela and asked how I was doing as a labourer in the woods, he unexpectedly added, "If someone wanted to know what we talked about, tell them that I asked you about the apple tree I had planted in your garden. I don't want to lose my pension, you know!"

There was also Verka Bohacova, still one of the closest of the Teleci congregation, who came in panic to tell me what she had heard in the factory she worked at. They were preparing 'my end'. (It probably concerned withdrawing my state preaching licence.) Verka was so terrified that she refused to come in and gave me all the 'top secret' information outside in front of the manse. Anybody could see her talking to me. She was aware of this and wanted to leave but could not. My prompting, "Go now," had no effect.

The presence of our four children was a great support too. They clearly had an effect on the conduct of those who came to take me away or ask questions. It was also good for us to be involved in the children's everyday concerns, which pointed to life beyond the eavesdropping madness. The children could also do unexpected things. Once, when the manse was under surveillance, we suddenly heard children's voices in our garden. Our children had brought their friends from school in over the back wall.

And it was through our family circle, the circles of our friends and the Teleci congregation that, in a very palpable way, we felt the presence of the One whose power has always been hidden but totally obvious. No, it was not possible simply to count on it nor point to it. But we often 'saw his back', the hem of the garment of the Almighty who was who he was and has remained the same until today. Evil enters our lives in many different forms and presents itself as omnipotent. And yet, if we can fully trust in the One who is mightier than that and if we do our best, we will be able to cope. Our trust in his power and help is not based on one incident, such as seeing a tiny microphone in the rough whitewash of the ceiling when we could never have imagined such an eventuality. Neither is it based on 'seeing only the back' of the One who has walked past unexpectedly. Rather it is inspired and sustained by all our life experiences and the trials we have been led through by him alone.

Had the Lord led us into a mine field? And did he leave everything up to us from then on? Certainly not! I don't remember that Daniela and I talked about it much. Today, after years of living together, we are more open in what we say to one another. But at that time, our being economical with what we said was also caused by the situation itself. The pressure did not ease. The summonses and questionings by the State Security gradually took on a more threatening form. Living constantly in strangely provisional circumstances consumed the energy which we needed for meditation and prayer. I still worked as a preacher and pastor of a congregation and my tasks were never-ending, which meant that I needed to keep reassuring myself and others too of God's power and grace. I had to try to find the confidence that God held our lives, the life of the congregation, of the community in the village and also the whole world, in his hand. This task was greater than the struggle of Charter 77, which we saw as an expression of what was missing in society at that moment.

It was clear that neither the elders of the congregation nor our friends were choosing to keep their distance from us. Therefore the authorities had to satisfy themselves by exerting pressure on our family; that is, on me. They would frequently summon me for questioning. They regularly threatened me and they kept suggesting that we should emigrate. Once, I was summoned to the district offices and both the vice-chairman of the district and the government clerk for the supervision of churches rebuked me for not having attended elections and for sympathising with my colleague Jan Keller, whose state licence had just been revoked. I pointed out to them that Jan Keller hadn't been given any reason why the measures had been taken. Expressing criticism towards the state authorities was unacceptable. They concluded the session with a threat that my salary would be adjusted according to my attitudes. Yes, they unashamedly said that my pay would depend on what I said. They wanted me to be silent. It never occurred to them that I was always rewarded for speaking. I was in fact 'paid' for saying words that were to bring life - I was rewarded by the Giver of life.

The pressure led us to consider whether the congregation and the community in the village were not being burdened too much and whether it wasn't all too threatening for them. Sometimes it was all too obvious, as, for example, when friends from Erfurt in the German Democratic Republic came for a short visit. Police checks were immediately set up at both ends of the road going through Teleci and all passing vehicles were stopped and the drivers' documents checked. Who would like that? I thought of the tractor drivers from the local cooperative farm. I knew them all. When we finally went for a drive with our guests in the car, we were stopped and asked where we were going, and then had our papers thoroughly checked. The policemen took our friends' passports into their car and copied all their details. Only then, when the State Security knew who our visitors were, did the police checks disappear from the road. Years later, well after 1989, when our German friends received their Stasi files and sent us a copy, we saw that they had been questioned as friends of Charter 77 on their return to the GDR.

The Synodal Senior, Milan Hajek, visited the Teleci congregation in July 1979. On this occasion I told him about the congregation and the elders being constantly under pressure from the State Security and I suggested that he should perhaps start negotiating with the state authorities for my possible transfer to another charge. His immediate response was that at the moment that would certainly mean losing my state licence. As Brother Hajek exceptionally agreed to stay in the manse overnight, so that "the Biseks would not feel that he was keeping his distance from them", we had ample time to speak openly together. On Saturday evening we discussed our involvement in Charter 77 and his opinion that it was an absolute mistake. An irreconcilable argument ensued. On one side stood the concept of the peaceful message of the gospel and the transformation of the world through peaceful witness to Christ; and on the other side was the struggle for society, truth, and justice, which was a continuation of the efforts of Calvin and Jan Hus (John Huss). I could not accept what he said about Charter 77 being just a scrap of paper. Our voices kept rising and it all culminated in an expressive silence in which we parted for the night.

In the morning, Brother Hajek complained of a headache. But he managed the Sunday Service. He preached on the parable of the rich fool from Luke, chapter 12 verses 13-15. I made a note of several of the main points: "Christ's revolution originates inside. It touches our world, which means our hearts and consciences. We must beware of greed and be on guard that we do not exalt ourselves but point to life as a gift in which God's grace is manifest". After the service, he gave a talk on the topic "Preach the Good News", based on his New Testament theology. Hajek's emphasis on inner renewal was, in my opinion, spontaneous and clear. He demonstrated the absolute necessity to concentrate unequivocally on Christ, whose kingdom, as I understood from the context of the talk, "is not of the world" (John, chapter 18, verse 36). Even up to the present day, I haven't been able to accept that we, as followers of Christ, might not feel part of the world. And here I see the "great *cloud* of witnesses" to Christ, past and present.

I didn't see his talk as an unfriendly act. On the contrary, I felt that he, in spite of being opinionated, was keen to be open in crucial matters. He didn't try to silence us. He just did not suppress his own way of thinking, which led him to react to a hostile regime in a different – conciliatory, almost appeasing – way. Of course, the problem was that the pressure of the state authorities was excessive and aggressive, which greatly diminished the trustworthiness of Hajek's attitude because, as I thought, being positive towards a brutal and hostile regime was questionable. I remember how I felt some sadness that we had not been able to overcome our differences. I also felt some regret at how lost Brother Hajek seemed to feel in his position of responsibility, which consumed him. We did not part in an unfriendly manner, quite the contrary. And after I had my state licence revoked, I saw how he tried not to neglect any opportunity to try to obtain a new one for me.

Our visit to Brother Hajek's retirement home after the Velvet Revolution in the early nineties was extraordinary. He touched on the argument we'd had in Teleci some twelve years before and also his own stance then. With sadness he remarked that he had been deeply mistaken and that there was no time now for him to change sides, as that would be too 'cheap' in the new era. Pleased, I commended the two of us to the grace and forgiveness of God.

The State Security were ready to take full advantage of our differences. Today I know that our argument in the Teleci manse was bugged. In the interrogations that followed Hajek's visit, the disagreement of the Church with my attitudes and those of some of my colleagues became yet another topic, as they pointed out how isolated we were and how our stance was meaningless and leading nowhere.

During interrogations the State Security tried hard to demonstrate how far-reaching their knowledge of my family was, and so they mentioned my sister living in India. The comment was racist and I was offended and stopped communicating with them altogether. The pair of State Security men who were questioning me had a twisted picture of the Third World and did not notice my being upset. After a while, though, they asked a direct question, "What's the matter, Mr

Bisek?" I did not respond. "Are you not well?" they continued. "Yes, I'm sick of you! I'm not going to respond to your offensive remarks about India and my sister!" I said. They tried to apologise, "Come on, you're being oversensitive! O.K., we're sorry". Now I am trying to figure out whether they had only a limited repertoire of threats and mockery or if my taking offence at something that was a digression from the investigation was too unexpected for them to cope with. They were certainly surprised at my resentment.

There was another unusual situation which I remember. One of the interrogators introduced himself as the chief officer. I had no idea why. But he put his questions to me in such a way that I considered whether he might have been authorised to arrest me. He was probably also showing off because, quite out of the blue, he asked if I wanted coffee. I said I did and in a short while somebody brought in three cups and placed them in front of each of us on the round table. The questioning continued. I took my time to react. Suddenly, the chief officer said, "Aha!" and started turning the tray around. I was surprised and said, "You seem to be trying to demonstrate that all three cups are safe to drink! You know very well that if I end up in prison I won't be able to choose what to eat and drink". He looked surprised too and did not respond.

So that was an account of how my 'visits' in Svitavy would go. They robbed me of my time and concentration and my courage kept diminishing. At the same time, I learned to rely on God, the ultimate source of the values which we had been trying erratically to hold on to. After every session I also had a feeling of frustration at the inadequacy with which I had dealt with my powerlessness. I was deeply dissatisfied with myself.

Most of the questioning sessions were on a 'local' level, in Svitavy. But there was one in Brno, and that was a dramatic experience for me, followed by 'local' repercussions. On several occasions I would go to Brno where the philosopher Bozena Komarkova organized meetings in her flat. About once a month Komarkova invited several dissident friends to discuss the current burning issues. These discussions were very encouraging for me and I still remember with great respect some of the participants and especially our host, Bozena Komarkova. Once the meeting took place in someone else's house. When it had finished and we emerged from the building, we were detained and taken to a police station. On the back seat in the police car I was sitting next to a colleague who had already lost his state licence and spent ten months in prison in the early seventies. He was rather desperately trying to get rid of some papers that were regarded as subversive. I saw it as futile, because it meant that either he or I would be found guilty of having possession of them. But at the same time, a free press was one of the basic rights that we, signatories of Charter 77, were trying to defend. Why was he doing it?

After getting to our destination we were separated. The interrogation that followed surprisingly did not touch on the question of freedom of the press. Anyway, the State Security in Brno gave me rather harsh treatment, because, as I thought, they wanted to demonstrate what they had the power to do. But on this Saturday evening my only concern was whether I would be released in time to get back to Teleci for the Sunday Service. I openly told them this although I knew that I was risking being held longer. If that was to be the case, they would be responsible for my absence at the Sunday Service.

In the end I got home in time. But the following week I received a special summons to go to the district procurator in Svitavy. There I was officially cautioned against anti-state activities and my finger and palm prints were taken. These were very dramatic moments, because I could not be sure that the papers left in the car in Brno didn't have my finger prints on them, although I had not touched them. I did not think that would have been a problem for the State Security. Would my protest against a State Security trick be heard? How would I defend myself? I didn't know what exactly had been left in the car. Why would I have hidden any papers when I always strove to act openly and freely? Would my ambivalence be interpreted as a sign of my inner disintegration? What would they do to me? – But nothing came of it. Were the times changing? Or else, were they being lenient because I was a minister known in the village and the district, in the church, among many friends and also abroad? I know now that they discriminated as they saw fit and they were quite capable of physically abusing and threatening those who were young and not well-known.

I have kept notes of the interrogations and below are some of the questions I was asked. They put my answers in writing and then forced me to sign the statement. I always found something to correct, either something factual or in the style or grammar. I was never given a copy of a statement and I wasn't allowed to take notes during an investigation. I wrote down what I remembered when I got home:

Have you met any foreigners lately? Who were they?

Who gave you thirteen thousand Tuzex vouchers?

Where and how did you sign Charter 77?

What do you know about the activities of the terrorist group Vejvoda-Taptuch, which was inspired and encouraged by Petr Uhl, whom you know?

How and when did you go to Vaclav Havel's place in Hradecek and who invited you?

You don't respect the regulations of the Synodal Council. Why?

Why do you criticise the Czechoslovak Socialist Republic and attack the government?

What do you know about the Committee for the Defence of the Unjustly Persecuted?

When did Vaclav Maly and Frantisek Lizna visit you?

What do you know about the Underground Movement and about the magazine 'Vokno' published by the group Starek, Fric, Jirous and Hribek?

How often and where do you meet Charlie Soukup and Stanislav Homola? What do they do?

What do Mr and Mrs Sabata do?

I would also be taken all the way to Hradec Kralove to be questioned. Once, they also took Anna Sabatova when she and her children were staying with us. The State Security men would appear unexpectedly in our hallway and say, "So let's go, Mr Bisek," and take me away. They would bring me back late that evening. The questionings in Hradec Kralove concerned people and situations I didn't know anything about. Therefore I refused to give them any answers, which stood in contrast with the 'local' interrogations in Svitavy, where I would acknowledge friendships with people they named and also refute their false allegations.

I was never able to predict what was going to happen and I was never sure in advance that I would be able to cope. I always tried to be very economical with what I said in response to their questions, because I wanted to avoid contradicting myself. My dissatisfaction and certain inner tensions were caused by my inadequacy in practical matters or debating skills rather than by wavering in what I stood for. On more than one occasion I felt I was being protected by God, who stands by the weak and those in danger.

It must have been due to all the tensions and my awareness of danger that I began to feel unwell. It reached such an intensity that I decided to go to a cardiologist at the clinic in Policka. He refused to see me at first as I had no referral from my GP. But I insisted and finally told him quite openly that because I had signed Charter 77 I was being constantly harassed by State Security. Then he examined me, told me that my blood pressure was too high and gave me pills. I was very grateful. I discussed this later with a doctor who once came late at night to attend to me when I was suffering from kidney stones. He remarked that a change of lifestyle would help. Neither of us knew how soon I would be working in the forest.

FAMILY PHOTO, 1982

Chapter 12

OUR PARENTS PASSING ON

The passing away of three of our parents happened at the time of increased harassment by the State Security. The first to go was Lydie, Daniela's mother, who died in December 1980. She had been our silent, unambiguous and constant support. In her I found encouragement and a clear involvement in my efforts at preaching. Both of us were fond of the Holy Communion service on Good Friday. It was a normal working day and so the congregation was smaller than on a Sunday. But the presence of Lydie was regularly an encouragement for me. She demonstrated for me her enjoyment of the community and the sacrament not long before she died. Her husband, Rudolf, wanted her to accept the bread and wine at a home Communion. In the strength of her humble faith she said, "But Rudi, I have already taken Holy Communion!"

She seemed to be able to feel the pressure of the authorities and understand the situation. I remember how she wanted us to cover the telephone with a pillow when we were going to tell jokes or speak about topics that might be interesting for the State Security. She also insisted on our hiding all unofficial printed materials, most of which were typewritten copies. It must have been due to her influence that I hid Charter 77 materials in the attic - as it so happened, just next to the eavesdropping device planted by the State Security!

Frantisek, my father, died in October 1983. He often came to visit us in Teleci and would stay for several days or even a couple of weeks. He, 'big grandfather' as the children called him, liked the company of his four grandchildren and enjoyed pottering in the garden or the shed. But he was always a little impatient to get back to Prague, so that my mother would not be on her own for too long.

When he suffered a stroke I went to see him in one of the Prague hospitals. There I had a rather unbelievable controversy with the ward sister. When I said who I was and that I had come to see my father she said that I could not see him and explained, "Your father is not reacting. Your visit, unfortunately, is pointless".

"But he's my father! Let me see him, please. I want to see him!"

"Don't you understand? You can't see him. He wouldn't know you anyway. And you don't need this".

"Don't be angry, please, he's my father and I must see him".

She gave me the number of the room and left without saying another word. The room had two beds in it. I recognised my father right away. He was breathing but did not react when I talked to him. In the other bed was another patient and at first sight I knew that he was not of Czech origin. He started talking to me but not in Czech. He spoke in English, which was clearly not his mother tongue. And so we talked together, each of us in our own English. He said, "Is he your father? He's very kind. I am from the police force in Kabul in Afghanistan. I was wounded when on duty and your country has offered to treat me". He extended his hand to shake mine and I wished him a speedy recovery. He added a few more words about my father, "We're here together. Your father does not speak but now and then he looks at me. I don't know if he recognises anything. I hope he'll get back home again." I thanked him and then bent down to my father, said a few words and passed on greetings from everybody. He did not react. I kissed him, said good bye to the Afghan policeman and left. My father died a few days later.

A few months after this, in March 1984, Rudolf, Daniela's father died. He loved coming to see us and found it easy to relate to the children, perhaps thanks to his profession as a paediatrician and also his experience with his own four offspring. He liked to play outdoor games and never tired of organising them when we had family reunions. But not everybody enjoyed croquet, one of his favourites! He relished our living in the manse because he loved the church and had been an elder for many years. I always grew nervous when it seemed that he took everybody in the village as a potential member of the church, asking passers-by to join the worshippers. He liked to repair faulty switches or door handles and wanted me to be his assistant, which I didn't like at all, mainly because I didn't have the time. He was unhappy when he couldn't find something he had brought into the house believing that it might become useful at some point in the future. I remember raking through the rubbish heap and looking for something Rudolf desperately wanted!

The children like to remember how the two grandfathers were in charge of them when we went to Brno for the day to celebrate our fifteenth wedding anniversary. Normally 'big grandfather' was very kind and lenient and grandfather Rudolf was strict. But that day the grandfathers' usual roles somehow reversed and to the children's surprise Rudolf read them a bed-time story and big grandfather chased them back to the bathroom to wash their feet properly!

The passing away of Daniela's parents was harrowing because of the circumstances of their deaths. Lydie died of aggressive breast cancer and severe side effects after radiotherapy. Rudolf had suffered from diabetes and died of embolism after amputation of a leg. The painful partings with our dear ones made us less sensitive to the aggressive attacks of the government officials and State Security. Now it seems to me that thanks to this experience, the framework of our life became much broader and, I would say, also deeper, so that being attacked by people we didn't know who were hostile towards us was not able to destroy it.

In this account of losing our children's grandparents I also recall the death of my mother in February 1989, nine months before the Velvet Revolution. In spite of having been expelled to Scotland, I applied to the Czechoslovak Embassy in London for permission to attend my mother's funeral in Prague. My request was declined by return. I complained about this to Norman Hogg, our MP in Cumbernauld. He acted on it immediately and about sixty Members of Parliament signed a petition on my behalf which Mr Hogg delivered to the Czechoslovak Embassy.[1] It was to no avail. I was not allowed to be present at my mother's funeral.

Some time later Mr Hogg told me sarcastically that the only result of his interceding was that in future he wouldn't be invited to receptions at the Czechoslovak Embassy. I had to tell him how sorry I was about his tough luck. I also told him that I didn't understand why my request had been declined. It must have been due to the rigid bureaucracy. It would have been simple to allow me to go, and once I was there they could have harassed me and given me a hard time. Neither of us knew then how close to its end the regime was.

---

1 See Appendix 4, page 199.

Chapter 13

THE END OF MY MINISTRY, AND FOREST LABOUR

It was spring 1982. The regional government clerk, Mr Kamenik, must have felt that my end was coming. One morning, a car stopped in front of the manse and he came to see me on a private matter. He said, "Mr Bisek, after all the negotiations we've had with you, the time to withdraw your state licence is almost here. It is unavoidable. I came to explain to you that, unfortunately, you'll see my signature on the document".

He waited for my reaction and I said, "And what do you expect from me, Mr Kamenik?"

"I just wanted to tell you that my signature does not mean that it was I who made the decision".

"What does that have to do with me?"

"Mr Bisek, I wanted to tell you that I don't decide these things."

"Why are you telling me?"

"I think you know what I mean."

"If I understand you correctly, you want me to look over your shoulder and try to see someone else who actually decides what happens to me? I can only say that it is you who bear full responsibility for your signature and no one else."

"So you don't understand me and you won't accept my explanation?"

"No, I don't, and I won't understand it in any other way."

"In that case we can't find common ground," he said and I replied, "No, we can't".

Mr Kamenik left. Extraordinary! we thought. And the devil smirked at us saying, "You see, you pathetic signatories! What is a signature?"

It was then that the Synodal Senior, Brother Hajek, suggested that it might be worthwhile to try for a transfer to another charge. I agreed and very soon received an invitation to apply to Horice, a small town in the north-east of the same region as Teleci was. That was on 16th April 1982. I responded by return of post and on 26th April the Synodal Council applied on my behalf for a preliminary state licence which was needed for my prospective election in Horice. A few days later I received a summons over the telephone to be at the District Council in Svitavy in the morning on the following day, 29th April 1982. When I got there, the regional clerk, Mr Kamenik, the district clerk, Mr Loukota, and the Moderator of the Presbytery, Mr Vyborny, were expecting me. I was officially handed a sheet of paper with Mr Kamenik's request that I should be transferred away from the region. It was dated 28th April 1982. The heading read, "The withdrawal of the state licence valid for a post of minister as of the 1st June 1982". The regional clerk mentioned the reasons the state authorities had for this decision, but I wasn't given any explanation in writing. The clerk said, "Mr Bisek would neither stop his activities in Charter 77 nor his friendships with those against whom he has been cautioned by the district procurator." I remember the monologues of the clerks and the Moderator that followed. Enlightened, I left without a word.

It is with pleasure that I read again the reaction of the Teleci elders addressed directly to the Ministry of Culture of the Czechoslovak Socialist Republic. In the letter they expressed their disapproval of the withdrawal of my state licence for Teleci and they asked the office to revoke the decision. They also said that their minister, Tomas Bisek, had their full support. The letter finished with these words: ". . . With regret we see this decision as a discriminatory measure against the Church and against our Teleci congregation . . ." Josef Dvorak, the session clerk and his deputy Antonin Lamplot signed the letter on behalf of the session.

The Synodal Senior, Mr Hajek, also wrote a letter on the instructions of the Synodal Council. It was addressed to the Ministry of Culture. His argument against the decision to withdraw my state licence was that Horice was far enough from Teleci but because it was in the same region the transfer could be managed before the 1st June 1982, when my licence was to expire. If the Ministry could not agree, Mr Hajek requested that the deadline at least be extended, so that a congregation in another region could be addressed. Alarmed, I read again Hajek's proposal by which the state authorities' plan to extract me from the community of my brothers and sisters would be fulfilled.

Here too it's the devil turning round and jeering. He hisses, "Off you go on your own. It's your Exodus!"

The reply from the Ministry was negative. It only stated that the decision to withdraw Mr Bisek's licence was well within the law which had been valid since 1949, that there was no legal right to have a state licence, and therefore no basis for the request to grant Mr Bisek a state licence for Horice.

I never discovered what exactly I had done to have my licence revoked. My ministry in Teleci ended. I preached my last sermon on Pentecost Monday, the 31st of May 1982.

OUR LAST SUNDAY IN TELECI

It was clear that those in power intended to annul my influence in the community that had been supporting us. The most effective way would be to make us emigrate. This suggestion had been put to me since 1976. Or else, we should at least disappear somewhere into anonymity. We felt that without some change our situation would become difficult to bear. I became unemployed on the 1st June 1982. It was a legal requirement to be employed. We hoped we would be allowed to continue living in the manse, because there was no other place where we, a family of six, could go.

Fortunately, we weren't left without help. It came from our friend Pavel Roubal, who had some experience of losing a job. He explained to us that the legal requirement to be employed could be fulfilled by going to the district employment office where they were obliged to offer jobs to unemployed citizens. I went to the Svitavy Employment Office immediately and asked to be put on the job seekers list. The woman at the desk explained her refusal to put my name down by giving me a list of jobs available at the moment. My eye was immediately drawn to job vacancies in the Forestry Commission in Borova, because the area also covered the woods around Teleci. I told the woman that I hadn't found anything relevant to my qualifications. Her reply was, "That's your problem."

"All right", I said, "I'll think about it and come back."

When I got home, Daniela and I agreed that I might try to make my boyhood dream come true and plant saplings and do other unskilled jobs in the forest. I went to the Forestry Commission in Borova the next morning and spoke to a Mr Chaloupka, the forester. By his reaction he let on that he had heard about me. He didn't say they would not employ me. On the contrary, he said that nobody could object to them giving somebody a job which had been advertised and which nobody wanted to do. I just remarked, "You'd better be prepared that there are those who'll be keen to know what I'm up to."

"I understand and I'll inform Mr Klodner, our boss, who is a member of the Party. But I can't imagine he would object to you being taken on. He keeps asking if anyone has applied for the job."

Some years later I learned that Mr Klodner had been summoned to Svitavy, where he withstood the pressure of the State Security to cancel my contract. Legend had it that Mr Klodner was surprised that they could imagine that Mr Bisek might incite the trees in the forest to sign Charter 77!

Only a few days later, with my arms and back aching, I was planting saplings in a clearing near the village of Borova. I was very content, although at the back of my mind I was worried as to what the gentlemen who focused on my leaving Teleci would come up with next. This lasted for several weeks but then I chased away any anxiety about how I would manage because it was only the beginning of summer and there was no telling what might happen in the meantime. I also realised that the change in my lifestyle was difficult. I wasn't able to relish the satisfaction that Teleci remained our family home. Physical exhaustion had the upper hand.

The efforts of the Synodal Council on my behalf were surprising. I felt it was the Synodal Moderator's attempt to apologise for having misjudged the situation when he applied for my transfer to Horice and now he seemed to be trying to rectify it. I remember when we spoke together and I tried to comfort him saying that it had been State Security's doing that I'd lost my state licence; they had had the last word.

The Synodal Council's first attempt took us to Stramberk, a small town in the east, in the North Moravian Region. Daniela and I were immediately invited to visit Stramberk by the session of the congregation and we rather liked it there. A request for a preliminary state licence dated 9th July 1982 was followed by a summons and I was to be in Svitavy on 16th July:

"So, Mr Bisek, how do you feel about having your state licence revoked? And what is Mr Homola doing?" (Stanislav Homola was a signatory of Charter 77, who had moved to the area and we had occasionally met.)

"And what about Mrs Sabatova? It's high time you emigrated or else you must give us a one-hundred percent guarantee that you will change your attitudes. What do the members of the session say to your working as a forest labourer? It's a piece of nonsense, isn't it?"

A few days later the Synodal Council received a reaction from the regional government clerk in North Moravia. He rejected their request. I was sad but also grateful when a letter from Stramberk arrived in the middle of September in which the session expressed their disappointment and also encouragement.

Gradually I got used to my existence in the forest which was pleasantly brightened by a number of visitors who wanted to experience forest labour. These were not only the family but also friends. I remember some of them came from far away, like the minister of a German church, a couple from Switzerland and a musician from California. Our stout supporters were Dutch friends, especially those who had studied theology at the faculty in Prague. They kept offering help in the form of books or money. To my question as to whether their financial help was meant for people in the church they replied without hesitation that it was up to us. Once, when our Dutch guests had left to visit friends in a neighbouring village, we remembered that Anna Sabatova had mentioned that her husband Petr, at the time in high security prison, needed vitamin supplements. So I picked up the phone and told Mr Palat, who the Dutch friends were visiting, that we needed vitamins. He rang the next day to say that my axe had been sharpened and I should collect it from the collective farm warehouse where he worked as a storekeeper. A little while later, Mr Palat handed me an axe I had never seen before and an envelope with cash for Anna and Petr. This was how Mr Palat and our Dutch friends had 'deciphered' our request. Although their conclusion was logical, I had great difficulty in explaining that 'vitamins' was not code for cash. In the end, proper vitamins arrived as well.

Martin, a colleague from my studies at the Theological Faculty who emigrated after 1968 and worked as a minister in the Swedish Lutheran Church, arrived late one night, so that he would not be noticed. He said something that was very disturbing: a colleague of mine whom Martin had just visited had warned him, "Don't go to see Bisek! He'll have a hard time because of your visit and you'll never get a visa for Czechoslovakia again." This was exactly what the State Security wanted: to isolate us. The colleague's advice was disheartening, but Martin's independence was encouraging.

It was October 1982. The Teleci congregation got a copy of the letter which the Synodal Council had received from the regional clerk in Hradec Kralove in response to their proposed arrangements for the Teleci congregation during their vacancy. The regional clerk had come to an agreement with the interim Moderator, a colleague of mine, Josef Sladek, who was minister in the nearby town of Policka. At the same time he refused to give permission for Daniela to work as secretary of the congregation. The regional government clerk made the conditions very hard for Josef, who was supposed to manage both congregations without any other assistance. The regional clerk also said that no one would be granted a state licence for Teleci as long as the Biseks lived in the manse. The Synodal Senior wrote back to him to say that the Synodal Council was not going to evict us. It meant that we could continue living in the manse.

This we accepted with great relief. I felt for Josef, the interim Moderator. He belonged to the older generation and we, the younger ministers, always held him in high regard. He had been working on the ecumenical translation of the Old Testament for years. We were interested in it and so he always obliged and told us about the results of his research. On the other hand, he was over-anxious in relation to the state authorities and that consumed him. I became fully aware of this again many years later, after the Velvet Revolution, when I appeared on his doorstep on a frosty night in early January 1990. It was my very first visit. I said, "Good evening, Josef. It's very nice to see you after so many years. I'm sorry if I'm disturbing you, but I wonder if I could use your phone to make a call to Teleci, so that they could come for me. Otherwise I won't be able to get there because the last bus had left before the train arrived." Josef was overcome and said, "I meant to tell you all those years ago, Tomas, that you shouldn't have gone to Scotland. But I never did. It's never gone out of my mind. I'm really sorry."

Yes, Josef was right. It was true that we had never had a meaningful conversation when he was interim Moderator between 1982 and 1985. That was a failure by both of us. I had worried that I might complicate his work in Teleci, which was in addition to his responsibilities in Policka and also the translation of the Old Testament. I was always there but he would never ask me to help him out. After twelve years of ministry I sat in church like other worshippers. Josef and I met regularly – but just made small talk . . . I can only despair now at how effectively the authorities had us cornered.

Two of our close colleagues, Petr Brodsky and Bohdan Pivonka, sent out a letter to all vacant congregations in autumn 1982. In the letter they described our situation and encouraged the congregations to invite me as a candidate for their vacancy. In the next three years I received a number of invitations. It was a pleasing result. In some cases, depending on the situation, the Synodal Council applied for a state licence on my behalf. I managed to visit quite a few congregations. I saw different corners of Bohemia and Moravia, although sometimes just in the form of paperwork. These were the places: after Stramberk came Dankovice, Prestice, Opatov, Strmilov, Rusava, Rymarov, Nejdek, Trebenice and Hrabova. This effort, especially the involvement of the Synodal Senior Hajek, brightened my forest labour. We knew that we were not completely forgotten. Unfortunately, it became obvious that the State Security had my fate in their hands. But they did not have to interfere in Trebenice. The Trebenice session acted on their own initiative and asked us to visit them. Their former minister was a man of vision and had warned the Trebenice session against having me as their candidate, because they would be punished and not be allowed another minister.

The applications for a state licence that the Synodal Council sent on my behalf kept both the church and us hopeful, though they always ended in disappointment. The Synodal Senior hoped that a regional clerk willing to grant a state licence for me might be found. But the State Security machinery, supervising everything from the wings, had a clear plan. It was a gradual process by which 'object Bisek', as I was called in their file named 'Seclusion', should be driven to emigration. Every application for a state licence was followed by an interrogation. I was always requested to give them a hundred percent guarantee that I would give up all my activities, "or else, Mr Bisek, pack up and go to your providers. We'll be happy to assist you." Now, I have in my hand the judicial verdict on the principal State Security men which I received in the Nineties. It says that we were one of a number of families, about eighty people, who had been forced out of the country during a State Security operation which was called 'Clearance'.

Time moved on relentlessly and, depending on the season, planting saplings, drying birch leaves, or repairing forest paths came to an end. Finally Mr Chaloupka, the forester, came with a question, "Are you willing to chop off the branches from trees that your colleagues fell?" So I joined a small team of forest labourers. The looming winter did not interrupt my work. But it meant that I had to take an axe and start practising. I gradually got used to it but I found that whenever I tried to read a book, I would always fall asleep over it.

A permanent change to my work in the forest came with the weather getting colder. Late autumn brings difficulties for lumberjacks. My new colleagues found it a bother to have to walk from one place to another looking for trees to fell for me. Everybody had enough to do to fulfil the daily requirement of cubic meters of logs. They never complained to me, but I felt I was being a nuisance when I asked them to interrupt what they were doing and fell another tree for me, so that I could chop off the branches. Svata, our local Forest Warden, approached me and said, "There's nothing else for it. You'll have to fell trees too, boy. I can't be for ever asking the others to help you when they can't manage their own work. I don't know what to do with you."

I already knew that the regulations for work with a chainsaw were very strict. I expected that the forestry commission might send me on a course. Why not? So I said, "OK, I'll try. We'll see if I can manage." But there was no course. Instead, my first attempts at working with a heavy chainsaw were really difficult. I remember how it was sometimes almost beyond my endurance when a tree I tried to fell did not fall but the treetop got caught in the branches of another tree. Sometimes it happened due to it being the wrong direction, at other times because of my misjudgement of the density of the trees around. This was exactly what Svata had warned me against. He said, "No 'hangers', please." I learned the jargon of lumberjacks.

In the first months of working with the chainsaw Svata showed me thinner trees to fell. Gradually I joined the fellers' team and did my share of work. I noticed how we were all a little apprehensive. The forest had been their work place for years and I was new and different. I remember how I was slowly getting closer to Mirek Nemec, in fact the only colleague directly from the village of Teleci. It was important for us to work in close proximity to one another. The work regulations stipulated that a feller cannot work alone. There had been too many serious and even fatal accidents among forest workers – comparable to accidents in coal mines.

Mirek and I got used to working alongside one another and eventually became good companions. From time to time Pepik Dvorak and his horse did some pulling of logs and sometimes Mirek Lunacek from Breziny came on his tractor to tow away the heavy timber. That was our 'Teleci team'.

A tree feller learns very soon that work in winter is more taxing than in summer. When winter began, it was still dark in the morning. Sometimes we had to cover several kilometres to get there, often in snow up to our knees. To manage on the frosty days in the forest without a shelter van meant keeping a bonfire alive. I was able to cope with minus fifteen Centigrade. When it was colder than that and perhaps even windy, my fingers wouldn't stay flexible enough to work. When there was a van, Mirek and I had the chance to let our conversation wander beyond the cramped space and our forest. I remember Mirek's indignant comments about collections for the Third World. Mirek had his own view, probably formed by his circumstances. He said, "I wouldn't give a thing to those black bums. Yes, I wouldn't give anything to anybody. Nobody's ever given me anything." And he finished the thought in a rather interesting way, "Here, Tomas, would you like a bun?" His wife sometimes made delicious buns filled with plums, oozing with butter. I became an exception to Mirek's principle!

What his view of me, a minister turned lumberjack was, I heard from him just before Christmas 1984. We had a party round a bonfire at the end of the season. Quite a few people joined us and almost everybody had brought a bottle of alcohol. The last to come was Svata, our local Forest Warden. I knew already that he had a problem which had taken him to an alcohol rehab centre. He stood up and declared, "So, guys, Christmas is here! Be quiet! Everybody! Now! And you, Tomas, you stand here on this stump and preach!"

I waited to see what would happen. It was Mirek who reacted immediately, "You're nuts, Svata. We've had Tomas with us the whole year so we know what he thinks."

Did Mirek say that I had earned his respect? But Svata would not let up. He insisted on repeating, although now in a rather slurred way, "Shut up! And you preach!" But the others joined in, "Hey, Svata, you're a pain in the arse! Mirek's right!"

Svata's next words were too slurred to be understood. He sat down and took a mighty swig straight from the bottle. Then he bent forward, almost fell to the ground, got up and staggered away. I didn't have the experience of the others and so I asked, "Where is he going?" Somebody said, "Home".

I continued, "But not like that! He'll freeze somewhere in a bush, won't he?" Somebody said, "Don't worry, he knows his way. When he's steaming, he's like an animal. He feels the pull of home".

When spring arrived, we could sit at the bottom of a tree and let the sun's rays warm our faces. In summer we ate our sandwiches lying on the soft moss, looking up at the moving clouds through the green treetops. Then it was difficult to get up again, pick up the chainsaw and return to work. I should mention here that I never adopted the style of a real tree feller: at work a feller never puts his chainsaw down, he uses it also to strip branches off the trunk. The vibration of a chainsaw for a whole day has an effect on the hands. After years of working with a chainsaw, a tree feller can become disabled because of his hands. He needs regular check-ups to prevent this from happening. Every year we had to attend the local doctor's practice, where we had to put our hands and forearms in a basin filled with very cold water for some minutes. Then the GP would press our fingers and the palms of our hands, which were very painful from the cold water, to see if the blood would come back. But our GP wasn't very careful and left us to do the soaking without supervision. Mirek always cheated and kept adding a little hot water to make it bearable. To save my hands, I always put my chainsaw down and used the axe to chop off the branches and so the impact on my hands was reduced. On the other hand, I was less efficient than the others.

It must have been due to good luck rather than my carefulness that I had no accidents in those three years. I enjoyed showing people in the lumberjack's way that I had four children: I hid the two middle fingers in the palm of my hand, put my thumb on them and stretched out my index finger and my pinkie, "Look, how many children I have?"

I had the pleasure of the company of my two sons, Lukas and Benjamin, in the forest too. And in fact, when I planted saplings and later felled thinner trees, the whole family would occasionally join me. The boys were always eager to help their dad. And Svata, the forest-warden, tolerated them. What a view of health and safety at work! Sometimes, when I was on my way home in the afternoon and came to the slope opposite the manse, I could hear shouts of greetings and see small figures running down the hill from the manse and then up again to meet me.

But the forest did not save me from my guardians. On the anniversaries of the occupation in 1968, or whenever the Synodal Council applied for a state licence on my behalf, or sometimes just because I should not forget that they knew about me, I would get a summons for questioning. I remember how once, just before 21st August, I didn't feel well in the morning and so I decided to go to work a little later. On that day they appeared in our hallway and asked Daniela where I was. She pointed to the forest and they left. We knew they would be looking for me, so I set out immediately for the forest. But I wasn't sure how to get across the road in my bright orange overalls. They would easily see me. So I walked at a steady pace, crossed the road and climbed the opposite slope. When I got to my spot in the forest, I felt relieved. At the time I was alone for a few days because I was working only with my axe and the regulations did not forbid it. I sat down and waited for them to arrive. But, of course, they could not find me. Only when I started working could they hear me. They arrived within minutes and said, "Where are you, Mr Bisek?"

"What do you mean where? Here, in the forest, as you can see."

"OK, pack up your axes and let's go."

A small victory? Not at all. I was like a mouse that grinned because it hadn't yet been caught, but knew very well that it could happen at any time.

The last application for a state licence for me was written in August 1984. It was for me to work in Hrabova, a village in North Moravia. The Synodal Council had considered this option for a long time. But again, it was rejected. I sensed that the Council's disappointment at the set-back was ominous. A letter of 22nd August 1984 from the secretary of the Synodal Council confirmed my foreboding. All the previous applications and dealings on my behalf were listed and the letter ended with these words: "The Synodal Council has explored every possible avenue." The last meeting I had with the Synodal Council took place on 18th September. Paradoxically, I was pleased to see the regret with which Brother Hajek concluded our quest. I didn't hear in it any reproach for my independent stance or for signing Charter 77. Everything was verbal, nothing was written down and Hajek gave me words of encouragement when I mentioned my intention to look for work in another church. And so the last leg of our family's quest began.

We knew then that our squatting in the manse was drawing to an end.

What next? First, our friends, Brona and Jiri Muller, arrived. In 1979 they had had their wedding ceremony and reception in Teleci which was attended by many signatories of Charter 77. They had visited us often and now came with an admirable offer: we could share a house with them. They'd thought it all through. They would find money to buy a property. They'd take care of everything. We found ourselves completely at a loss for words. It was very difficult to know how to respond. Their proposition was extraordinary. But on the one hand we thought about our four growing children, and on the other Brona and Jiri at the beginning of their married life. Another factor was that both our families had been under constant police surveillance. Moreover, I had already been nurturing my dream of continuing working in a church. To their grave disappointment we declined their kind offer.

Soon I had some encouraging invitations to work as a minister in a German or Swiss church. But thanks to our past experience of speaking English, and Daniela having lived in Scotland, we dared to hope that an invitation might come from that direction. That exploration was another, separate, part of my search.

Chapter 14

EXILE

I was told at the Synodal Council that they could do no more to get a licence from the Ministry of Culture for me to work for the Evangelical Church of Czech Brethren again. We had to decide what to do.

It was not easy to leave. I remember how we prepared for our move to Scotland – a kingdom of lochs and sea, bright greens, constant rain and peculiar Scottish people.

For example, we were only partly successful in taking our books with us. We had to take a detailed list to the Director of the regional library in Hradec Kralove. The lady librarian set to work without delay. She went through the list, item by item, and, with a red pencil, kept crossing out the books she considered objectionable.

"But they will disappear in the right direction and they won't confuse anyone any more," I tried to defend my books. The librarian responded without hesitation, "I know, I'm a butcher. But believe me; sometimes I do good work too. Nobody told me about any direction. My task is to cross out all forbidden books. Two comrades from the regional Committee of the Party will check my work. What can I do? I don't want to lose my job! I don't think I need to tell you more," she added. I did not expect her to.

What kind of books were forbidden? Particularly the writings of Tomas Garrigue Masaryk, Edvard Benes and everything concerning these two Presidents of Czechoslovakia before and during the Second World War. I was not able to understand this choice. By contrast she did not touch the books that were important to us and that we would class as 'objectionable'. They probably hadn't made it to the official list of forbidden books yet. One such book, in German, was by a Swiss church historian Professor Andreas Lindt from Bern, 'Das Zeitalter des Totalitarismus', in which he writes about the twentieth century as an era of totalitarian regimes. He demonstrates their deformity.

"Do you actually have a detailed list of forbidden books?" I asked the librarian.

"Yes, I'll show you," the librarian said.

After several hours of the 'butchery', we went home with my long list properly modified. It was really peculiar. I still have it.

Several months passed before the customs officers arrived to complete the episode with the books. Their task was to oversee our packing and then they were to seal everything, so that we would not be able to misuse our possessions!

"So where are the books that have been crossed out?" was one of the first questions.

"I've given them to my friends, because we're not allowed to take our own books with us," I replied.

"Did nobody tell you that you have to show them to us? Somebody's botched it again! What can we do?" they went on. "In that case we've got to go through the lot!"

They began working very carefully, keeping the family at a distance, as if we had an infectious disease. After a while, however, they accepted my assistance. And so I managed, thanks to this cooperation, to get a number of the forbidden books to Scotland.

Getting all the necessary formalities needed for entry into the United Kingdom was not free of complications. It started with a postcard from Fiona Hulbert. For necessary reasons the text was very brief and we had some difficulties in deciphering it: "Come to us. Write to Andrew Morton at 121 George Street." That was all! Nothing more.

MOVING FROM TELECI TO SCOTLAND

How could a lumberjack in Teleci know that Andrew Morton was the Europe Secretary at the central offices of the Church of Scotland in Edinburgh? I did not know, but learned what it meant in good time. It was autumn 1984 and a guest from Scotland was to attend a celebration of the Reformer Zwingli in Brno. It was a very rare occasion to have a visitor from Scotland and we were keen to see who he was, so we decided to attend the event. This was how we met the Revd Andrew Morton. We spoke outside in the rain. Several months later I was invited to work as an associate minister in Condorrat Parish Church, a Church of Scotland congregation in Cumbernauld.[1] This conversation had been decisive. The process of getting a permit to work in Great Britain could soon start. I thought that the negotiations would only be a formality. But it was not so simple. I was invited to meet the Consul at the British Embassy in Prague.

When I arrived, I first spoke with a friendly Embassy clerk who was responsible for welcoming visitors. Then the Consul took me to the inner parts of the building, to a big hall, in the middle of which stood something like a tent. I named it the 'Tent of the Covenant'.

We entered the tent and I was asked to sit down on one of the two chairs at a small table. That was all there was room for. The conversation in my 'Tent of the Covenant' went like this: "When and why was your licence revoked? Who are your friends in Great Britain? Where and when did you sign Charter 77? Can you name any other signatories? Who do you know from the Church of Scotland? Etc . . ."

It was obvious that my integrity was being tested in the tent. The conversation soon took a turn: "Once in London, would you like to be met by members of an organisation that helps political asylum seekers?" And, finally, "Why do you want to rely only on the church?" Yes, I did rely on the church, because I had been given reason to by the Church of Scotland, whose service I was going to enter. I saw no reason for taking the resources that others might need.

Some people obviously arrived in the UK with no support and no friends, no qualifications and no knowledge of the language. Yes, there were many who were uprooted when they arrived and brought with them only their confusion and a trust that they would be helped. It was never simple and never would be . . . We would have to try

---

1 See Appendix 2, page 196.

to overcome the distress and misery of the past and hope that new horizons would open up.

What was the tent where I got permission to enter Britain? I did not dare to ask. I told myself that it was a place where the big ear could not reach: the ear that served the Czechoslovak regime to hear what could be either useful or dangerous. I was tested in the tent and the trauma of our move got dangerously close.

How did we manage to leave home? I should first mention that Daniela and I, the parents of four children between ten and fifteen years old, thought that although they were not old enough really to appreciate what it meant to emigrate, we had to talk about it all together. We were no wiser than they were. Who knew what we might lose through emigration? Who could appreciate the consequences of a step which was so far from the ordinary? We were very keen that the family circle be united somehow.

After a court hearing the children were allowed to keep their Czech passports, unlike us, who had to relinquish our citizenship. But we promised that if they were allowed to return home, we would not stop them. To our surprise, the children chose to spend all their summer holidays and then even Christmas in Czechoslovakia.

Now I am going to take you with us on our journey. First we drove from Teleci to Prague for the last time. We stayed with Lydie, Daniela's sister, and her husband Pavel. There was a big farewell party in the garden with at least forty friends to celebrate Holy Communion together for the last time and see us off.

The last evening was not without excitement. At the beginning of July 1985, there was a gathering of the Christian Peace Conference in Prague. I still maintain that I did not think it was relevant for me. I had never had anything in common with these peacemakers. However, I could never have anticipated what actually happened: the British delegates were to be on the same flight as we were! They were going home; we were leaving home.

The British delegation started to swarm around us as soon as they spotted us at the airport. Somebody had told them about us and they hastened to tell us that they would be our personal protectors should we have any more trouble with the Czech police 'minders'. They created quite an atmosphere of care and protection in the face of the dangers of the world!

Was it advantageous? Probably yes, I thought. On the other hand, it was also rather alarming. Even today I am not sure if I would have done it that way. It was obvious that they had no time to become aware of our inner trauma. We were beginning to feel the gnawing pain that marked the beginning of our exile, the feeling of loss, separation and even betrayal. Our feelings were too complicated to resolve. Was it something we were going through because of a previous decision, or something that had already happened? It was one of those moments in my life when I felt strongly how much I was at the mercy of the situation; I was not able to see clearly and react appropriately. For Daniela and me, it was a moment when we were in need of prayer; we needed to be reassured that there was One who would listen. But there was no time. The children had been left completely on their own, with their own thoughts and uncertainties.

During the flight I kept answering questions put to me by Canon Kenyon Wright, President of the Christian Peace Conference. He was eager to be reassured that the Christian Peace Conference was a good thing. But I could not give him any such assurance. 'In return', Canon Wright was not able to get us through the passport barrier at Heathrow Airport. I felt sorry for him.

The passport officer saw that our permit to stay in the United Kingdom was for 365 days. Where would people with no nationality go at the end of the year? We had to wait for three hours before a phone call to the Home Office decided that we were allowed to enter. Confused, we stepped onto the territory of Her Majesty. What would happen next?

We were in London. To begin with I felt relieved that the country of our destination was our own choice. However, it was a strange 'freedom'. With time we received the relevant documents which allowed us to travel "anywhere in the world except Czechoslovakia". We could not go home . . . But I am jumping ahead.

We were still on our journey. Where were we then? We saw the huge airport with a lot of different signs, and flashing lights coming from all directions. There were crowds of people who seemed to know where they were going; people who appeared to be sure of what they wanted. All that made us feel even more helpless.

No, we were not completely forsaken. There were friends who received us with open arms. They had waited for us for three hours. They did not abandon us in our first steps; any previous experience in the country was useless at that time. To arrive, settle down and live there was not the experience of a tourist. It was not an experiment. A romantic urge to be curious and compare the new with what was familiar dissolved very quickly. It was not a trip. We were not there to accumulate impressions which would entertain others.

And so, first of all, how did we communicate? I had wrestled with English before and Daniela perhaps a little more than I. We had gathered some experience. But still, London was full of a foreign language. It could not have been otherwise. And of course, there was a completely different atmosphere; the customs and reactions of people were strange. London did not seem to be just one huge city; it was a conglomeration. We saw advertisement after advertisement, a complex traffic system, taxis and buses, the underground and buildings and houses, so much of the same and yet still surprisingly different. In contrast, next to all the bustle, there were parks with their peacefulness. No one seemed to be in a hurry there. What about us? Should we not hurry? Were we allowed not to have to hurry? How were we to find some peace?

London was not my home and therefore I probably felt that everything was fuzzy and confused. There was a haste and restlessness which I could not understand

But let me stop and say again that there were friends who upheld us. They put us up, and before giving us a bed they made everything seem as it should be. The confusion was only an outward appearance. Behind it we would discover a new order which was meant to calm us down and comfort us. But I was not sure yet if it would be possible. In the morning, tired and worried, but still excited and full of expectations, we boarded a train to take us to Scotland.

The train was taking us north. We tried to imagine that we were going home. Now, when we remember it, we can indeed say that Scotland, at first a foreign country with people we did not know, did become our home. During the first journey, however, we had to try to convince ourselves. Yes, we were going somewhere where our home would be.

We were to live in a new town which we had heard about from Czech friends who had seen the plans. They were both architects and told us about a town where cars and pedestrians did not meet. It was a satellite town where people from rundown neighbourhoods of Glasgow could move and start life afresh. Many were intoxicated at having a new house. And yet, to me it was no more than a humanised variation of the Stalinist megalomania, which erased the dirty stains on the faces of modern cities quickly and effectively. It is interesting how the pride of a master creator, reshaping the world like that, spread on both sides of the Iron Curtain. It spread in all directions. How else could so many uniform solutions for the poor of Europe come into existence right across the continent? That was something, however, we were not interested in at the time. We had enough to do with our own dreams and fears.

I like the railway and always think of travelling by train as a reward no matter what experiences it comes after. The railways used to be the national pride of Britain, so I'm told. Hearing a train meant that you could set your watch. You could drink tea from china cups on the train, certain that it wouldn't spill! The rapid and aggressive development of motoring and the preference for the road over the railway has turned the railway into a Cinderella. Now it is like a doll without a head, without arms and with only one leg, thrown into a corner. Today you can see cyclists, couples, parents pushing prams, walking along disused railways in Scotland. And what still remains and is in use is far from the punctuality of yesterday, let alone the comfort of times gone by.

We were on our way. It was a rainy day but we could still see the flat English countryside, rows of identical houses, advertising hoardings, fields with cattle and parks with tall scattered trees. We knew that in a few hours we would see the hills of the Scottish Borders. We fought our tiredness and tried to imagine the open arms of our new and unknown friends. We did not talk about what they would be like, but we all hoped that they would be friendly and understanding.

Chapter 15

OUR NEW HOME IN SCOTLAND; ADJUSTMENTS

At the Theological Faculty in Prague, Professor Rican's lectures on history were not brimming over with everyday reality. He was, probably, too cautious, too 'dry'. He would not venture anywhere where he felt unsure; as if his awareness of the limits of what he knew stood in the way. Only now and then he would add a comment, which was, usually, vivid and appropriate. Once he told us how, at the beginning of his studies in Glasgow, he went for a walk on a Sunday. He got as far as Glasgow Central Station. In the spacious hall of the station, which he knew very well, he heard a regular clicking as he walked. He stopped, listened and looked around. There was complete silence. He started walking again and realised that what he heard was the clicking of his heels. Of course, it was a Scottish Sunday: the Sabbath, in a country where the Reformation had made its mark. Not so today! A Sunday in Glasgow is busy. Everyone goes shopping. Not only to accumulate things, it is a lifestyle, a way of spending leisure time.

And there we were, arriving at the 'clicking' Glasgow Central. A brief welcome by a small group of elders from our future congregation was followed by getting into the waiting cars which took us to Cumbernauld, a town about fourteen miles from Glasgow. In Balloch-Eastfield, in front of our future home, a truck was already waiting. It had brought our things from Teleci and had arrived two hours before us. Everyone carried our things in and immediately we were off again in the same cars to a restaurant for a welcome dinner. Who amongst our hosts could have foreseen that the newcomers would begin to fall asleep almost immediately? There couldn't have been much of a conversation. I don't remember how we got back 'home'. Then, finally, we were on our own. I remember well the sensation of tiredness mixed with anxiety and amazement that we were there: how could we be expected to feel at home and what should we actually be doing?

Our new home was a terraced house, with a small garden at the back, in a winding street bordered with patches of green and connected to similar streets by footpaths. Balloch-Eastfield was built in the style of a simple fishing village, so that it would be acceptable to those who came mainly from bedraggled tenements in Glasgow.

What we had brought with us was, in fact, superfluous. We were to settle in a new and completely prepared home. It had been fully furnished by the members of the Condorrat Parish Church. Balloch-Eastfield was a preaching station. They accepted us – six pigs in a Scottish poke. What would come of it? The first chapter of our assimilation in Scotland began.

On the island of Islay people say, "Tomorrow is too soon". I realise now that Islay would have been the best place for us to begin in Scotland. The Canada geese that come to the island in overwhelming flocks and eat everything in the meadows and fields, would agree. The farmers' guns which threaten them are mostly silenced by the law and so the geese, I am sure, take Islay almost as an ideal place.

And how would we take to Islay? The ever present wind and the Gaelic language would not always be so strange. Moreover, the Gaelic of the native speakers pleasantly inflected their English, which all of them were able to speak. In comparison with the torrent of Glasgow speech with all its 'colloquial creativity', English on Islay flows at a speed which is soothing and pleasantly reassuring: "You see, you understand something. You are only a little dim. No need to hurry, there's plenty of time!"

Cumbernauld offered a very different environment. It lies between Glasgow and Edinburgh, in the part of Scotland called the 'Industrial Belt'. No, we did not see a slow way of life as on the islands off the West Coast of Scotland. Really, everything was coming at us as if we had been thrown into deep water; there was no waiting for us to be ready. There was a lot happening from the very first minute and there was too much of it for unprepared newcomers.

Our past was cut away from us. It hurt; sometimes a lot, sometimes a little less, until the velvet ending in November 1989. By then, however, our destiny had been sealed for eleven years.

"What shall we do with him?" This question of mine was also a question for my new Church, and it was voiced by the people responsible for me in the headquarters at 121. The conveners and

Balloch in Cumbernauld

secretaries were a little unsure about a minister coming from the Evangelical Church of Czech Brethren, from a village, from a forest. First they thought it would not work. Then, one of them, Thomas Balfour, suggested: "Let's throw him in at the deep end. Then we'll see if he can swim".

Was I able to swim? I do not know. Was I swimming on my own? Certainly not! All the family somehow managed to swim, but inside we felt as though we were drowning, accompanied though we were by the kind sympathy of our new friends and neighbours. We were drowning, though mainly in our hearts. The water was drowning our memories, our aspirations, our self-confidence but also our readiness to set out and integrate. Our willingness and determination to respond to those who wanted to help us was seeping away.

I will just add that I was labelled as a Church of Scotland minister with a Czech background. Two weeks after we arrived, I started to preach, went into schools, visited families and did all the other things my colleague and boss told me to do. Our children started attending the Language Learning School off Great Western

Road in Glasgow. They suffered from having their mother tongue 'torn out'. Daniela, whose English was the most fluent in the family, took care of us and in many ways eased the burden we were gasping under.

What should I say? I wish everybody could travel freely and decide where they want to live. At the same time, I hope that everyone who wants to leave their homeland has the foresight to see what it *might* all entail.

Many ministers say that the need for teamwork will soon be recognized. One minister will not be able to cover a large diaspora. Ministers will also want practical and spiritual support. This will make colleagues cooperate more in carrying the burden of Christ's vocation.

Is this a promising development? Is it a solution to the situation of falling numbers? Is it more than the imperative of the current situation? That, of course, depends on us, especially on those who will want to or have to cooperate. It is not easy, since a minister's job is not free from the tensions generated by sharing work, sharing authority, interpreting God's Word and then taking it into the heat of the day. It also involves sharing possible dilemmas in pastoral care, the joys and pains of others. And it is excellent if we can share the challenge of the Good News and work together.

But it is not easy. Faith is not an entirely communal thing although it should bring one into community. The demands of Christ's truth and love create a strangely sensitive environment which plays on personal feelings: questions of authority, dignity, one's own importance and what one does are all involved. I sympathise with those whom Jesus called hypocrites and I don't think I would be far away from them. For I long to be myself and use my individuality – the weight of my personality – without being put in the shade by someone else who thinks he or she is my close colleague. I know what the truth is, what is valid, how we should live, what today's society is like and where our relationships grate. I know! I am the centre of myself; especially in so to speak spiritual matters. Here I am a little humbled by the unquestioning obedience of Roman Catholic brothers and sisters, especially those in holy orders. The discipline of faith, the emphasis on tradition, the obedience to authority etc., are things I am not very sure about and cannot cope with well. On the other hand, I like to uphold what our Church, which has only one Head and which is part of the universal church, has recognised as valid.

My findings about team work are derived from my experience of being an associate minister with a Scottish colleague in a growing congregation for almost five years. I found that he and I were diametrical opposites.

Our getting used to one another was often marked by the differences in our two worlds. My family arrived in Scotland as if handicapped and also, in a way, like poor relations who had been pushed out of their national nest.

"O.K., but how come that you've brought your own piano?" someone might have asked. A lot of books arrived with us too although they had been sifted through a strange ideological sieve. We arrived in Cumbernauld with £45 and did not know if it was a lot of money or a little. We were often clueless and yet it was very difficult to help us with a good piece of advice, which must have been frustrating.

My colleague was a bachelor. He had served the church for almost twenty years and was no novice. How could he then tolerate that these newly arrived parents, instead of responsibly calculating their spending ability, bought bikes for their two sons and even argued that they had to get the bikes as compensation for their miserable struggles with the language?

He often visited our house and found it difficult to accept that we spoke Czech with the children. He kept thinking about it and was worried. We weren't! We were not ready to give up our mother tongue. We only tried by looking at others in a similar situation to gather enough evidence and assurance that it was possible to keep one's own language. For us it was good and necessary. A mother tongue is more than verbal communication. Its place in the lives of all sorts of human communities is fundamental: a word can sometimes show extraordinary gentleness, sometimes gravity and seriousness, sometimes it can have a healing and liberating power. It is a gift beyond any other. May we not forget to whom we should be grateful for it.

However it was not only my colleague who struggled with our Czech. I remember an American woman, a theologian and the wife of a German minister who worked for the Church of Scotland. Immediately after the Velvet Revolution in 1989 she said to us, "You have no reason to be sentimental any more. Now you should only speak in English – at home as well!"

"No, we don't have to and we won't!" was our reaction. Really, it was not necessary.

It is well known that rejecting one's mother tongue restricts and impoverishes the intimate, emotional dimension which nourishes relationships.

My colleague was longing for the day when finally we would talk freely, from the heart, in English. Unfortunately, it did not happen, although in time we improved. You may ask, "How much did you improve? Be honest!" And I would say that in my opinion I entered the realm of a foreign language that will remain foreign till the end of my days. As if I got stuck in the gate.

Does it sound as if I am constantly in distress? No, I am not, because I keep learning how to reconcile my limitations on the one hand with the vast riches of a living language on the other, whatever the language might be. I remember an American linguist mourning when the last member died of an Indian tribe with whom he had engaged. He was sad because we, the whole human race, were the poorer for it.

> When the mother tongue falls silent
> An orphan's heartbeat you hear
> And in spite of the sun's rays
> Your own self you fear.
>
> The audacity of leaving
> Seizes hold of your heart
> And in hope you're wondering
> If you'll for ever live apart
>
> Only faith
> Restores one on the roam:
> Reconciliation with all
> In our Father's home.
>
> *Tomas Bisek, December 1987*

Tell me, how can we find harmony when there is friction? How can we reach such an understanding that we know our differences do not mean the end of our relationship? My colleague put a lot of effort into teaching me to speak English properly. Of course, it was Scottish English to a certain extent. It was appropriate, acceptable, and, in fact, interesting for me, although I did not think I had a choice. He also tried to tell me what to do so that we would complement each other in our preaching. This was less acceptable for me and, sometimes, I deliberately misunderstood, and I stumbled. We never spoke about it openly, but I felt that he, perhaps subconsciously, would have liked me to adopt his style.

In his sermons my colleague tried to exalt God's majesty and point to God as being set apart. He preached with feeling and rhetorical devotion.

I was, of course, immeasurably far behind in the language. I would like to say 'far behind him', but the matter was, surely, far broader than that. Also my ears were not yet accustomed to the language and I could not make out a lot of the words.

It might have been that I was not able to hear them. Or might I, sometimes, not even have been listening? I was not able to express myself as I would have liked to. I remember how I felt that I was speaking as it were, in an alienated way: it was not me but someone else inside me and, at the same time, beside me.

I felt compelled to slow my colleague down, to change his attitude towards me. Yet before trying to do that, I thought I should perhaps 'account for' what I have always felt called to do. However, it was too hard; my being fearful was also accompanied by a feeling of resentment. For several weeks, deeply unhappy, I would write my sermon 'homework' in my English. My colleague would come to see me on a Friday, read through it, change it, rewrite it and also read it aloud – as it should be. Then on Sunday, somehow I delivered the sermon at two out of the four preaching stations where Sunday services took place every week. As we partially rotated, there were some weeks when I did not have to sweat over another sermon, because I knew that at the place where I was supposed to preach there would not be a listener who had already heard my half-finished product, completed by my colleague. In that odd week, I had time to try to consider what to do next.

When my colleague took a month's holiday, an elder from the congregation took charge of me and it was a very different experience. He fully respected what I had written. He asked me about every detail. We cooperated on the language aspect and put right the grammar, structure and logical arrangement. I began to see myself in a new and enlightened way. I saw that my proficiency in English was very limited, but I did make attempts at expressing something. When my colleague came back from holiday, I refused to return under his wing. I began to be a little more independent.

Today I say that becoming emancipated is natural and necessary. Let us ask why: I think that we are called into fellowship so that we may support and carry one another. That in itself is very difficult. Our faith and ultimately also its verbal expression, is and has to be ours alone, individual to us; it is not assignable or transferable. In other words, face to face with God, we cannot be standing behind somebody else.

Neither can we just pass by without being noticed, nor can we send someone else instead of us who will speak for him or herself and also for us. This is not how we relate to God, the Creator and Father, for he has a personal relationship with each and every one of us. Therefore he gave us life. He does not receive us as 'numbers'. We are to speak and act for ourselves in our relationship not only to him, but also to ourselves and to others.

I continued to learn. After some time a retired minister of the Church of Scotland offered to help me. By that time I had improved a little and we could communicate and converse more freely. I attempted to be more exact in expressing my reaction to a biblical passage in a language I had much less under control than my mother tongue. I faced the key question regarding my Scottish adventure again: "Can I really manage to transfer my understanding and experience of the Good News into a different language and cultural environment? Will I be able to do it?"

Chapter 16

A FOREIGN ENVIRONMENT

Living in a foreign environment, meeting strangers and, not always being able to adapt quickly brings with it little accidents, misunderstandings and surprises. About two weeks after our arrival my colleague said, "You'll be getting a car. The congregation is growing and we both need a car for pastoral visits and Sunday services."

Several days later we went to a garage where we received the keys of a Ford Fiesta and people wished me many happy miles of motoring without a breakdown. The car had come from Skye where another minister, who I did not know, had had it before me. I was the second Church of Scotland driver to use the car.

My colleague drove it from the garage back to Cumbernauld, but then it was I who was to drive it. At the same time it was explained to me that foreign driving licences had only a limited validity in the United Kingdom. My colleague said, "You'll have to sit a driving test. British Traffic Law requires that your ability to drive on the left-hand side and your knowledge of the Highway Code be tested."

It was a worry for us since, we were told, only about fifty percent of candidates passed their driving tests in those days. People were very keen to tell us how difficult it was. However, my colleague recommended a very good driving instructor who knew all the local examiners and who would also tell us what exactly was to be learned. He comforted us, "You know how to drive anyway, don't you? It's only a performance of the proper way to drive."

Then he taught us our routines. I remember how he, an active Roman Catholic, advised me before the test, "Don't forget the routine which we've practised. I'm glad you're a minister. If you say a wee prayer before turning the ignition on, all will be well!" I never told him that I acted like a pagan. I passed the test although I had quite forgotten to say my prayer. Would it have any eschatological repercussions, I wondered? Perhaps there are only pedestrian zones in the New Jerusalem. All six of us passed our driving tests the first time.

My colleague had some peculiar ways with me. When I first started to drive he would explain to me the difference between a traffic sign and an advertisement. At the same time he would tell me where to go. I remember a journey to the Royal Infirmary in Glasgow: approaching a roundabout, he said, "Exit at a quarter past!" I pulled in, confused, and looked at my watch to see when it would be a quarter past. Surprised, my colleague waited a while before asking me, "What's the trouble?" – "I'm waiting for the hand to get to a quarter past," I replied. "Don't be silly," he went on, "don't you know that a quarter past means that you take the last exit? You just keep going round."

I had been used to consulting a map and I would have liked to use one to remember the way. However, my colleague did not like it and wanted me to remember the way by road signs and landmarks. But I could not manage to drive on the left-hand side of the road and notice signs and landmarks at the same time. All was very new to me. Everything was going by very fast. When I drove on my own, I just took out my map and tried to find my bearings in my old clumsy way. These were really only games, rather than anything else. They did not set us against one another. It was just teasing.

On one occasion I was like a little boy, really proud of where I had come from. My colleague and I were on our way home from the hospital in Coatbridge. It was cold and sleeting. I was driving my Fiesta. When we had left the town and there were only fields around us, the car stalled and would not go any further. My colleague remarked, "It's a pity it didn't happen in town. I don't know if we can get any help here." I was an unhappy driver whose car had broken down. So I got out and lifted the bonnet. My colleague got out too and asked, "What are you going to do? Are you a mechanic? You worked in the woods, didn't you? That's different, isn't it?"

I was listening to him and at the same time I fiddled with the distributor and spark plugs, saying to myself, "He's right. I'm a fool to be showing off like this!" We were wet and cold and got back into the car. In frustration I tried the ignition. The engine started and we were happy to be on our way home again. I was delighted and my colleague was very surprised. After some time I told him that in Czechoslovakia every driver had to be a mechanic as well or, at least, act like one.

This is how I would describe the initial period of our children's life in Scotland – life in opposition. They had not chosen the change they were going through. However, Daniela and I were very keen that they should agree to our leaving home and moving to Scotland. However, how could they accept something that was beyond their understanding, something that had disrupted their childhood and negated the experiences they had had so far? Everything was totally different for them. Of course, in general, any child's life is full of changes, because it is the beginning of life. On the other hand, from early childhood a child gathers experiences and certainties which are his or her support. When you take away the certainties, when you change the language, environment and people, when even the parents seem to react in a different way, it may seem to the child that everything and everybody is against them. All our children went through their pangs of change; they felt lonely and anxious because they did not know what would happen next. Some of the children at school seemed to be callous and almost cruel; our four were foreign and therefore not welcome.

This is how it was in the language school in Glasgow, where it was mostly Asian children who attended. After several months, our children gradually left and started in the local schools in Cumbernauld. The trauma of meeting a strange, foreign environment happened all over again, for each of them, now on their own. It would be too simple just to sigh and say that it was for their own good. It may have been so, but I would not recommend anything like it to anyone.

How then did the children react to all the changes? Certainly, each of them in their own way. There were, though, a few reactions which they had in common.

It was a bizarre surprise for us that they were allowed to travel 'home' to Czechoslovakia and nobody stopped them.[1] They had valid Czechoslovak passports, contrary to us. We parents had to get used to the fact that our children disappeared for the whole summer holidays and, later on, also for Christmas. We were happy for their time of bliss with all the extended family and friends. However, the result of these holidays in such a happy place was that Scotland, with school, language and all the strangeness, became a place of misery and waiting for the next journey eastwards. It got easier after several years when they each found their niche.

The two of us had to learn how to use the summer holidays on our own. During the children's absences we always enjoyed getting

---

1 See Appendix 3, page 198.

to know the beauty of the countryside and the interesting aspects of society in Scotland, England and Wales.

Cumbernauld was a place where people had moved to, mostly from Glasgow. The small houses with their tiny gardens made it look a little like the country. For us it was an environment where we would have liked to see hen houses, rabbit hutches and vegetable gardens as well. But there was nothing of the sort. You could come across these things in Scotland, but you had to go further north or south to the real countryside. People who had grown up in Glasgow did not see keeping animals and growing vegetables as something to do. We also discovered that there was no competition for us in looking for the gifts of nature and harvesting them.

There were, for example, wild mushrooms. The best samples of boletus were to be found in the Highlands. As if they were waiting just for us to pick them. Well, not just us. For example, a number of Poles lived in Dundee and we were told that Poles also knew about picking mushrooms. South of Dundee was Tentsmuir Forest Park, where we did not mind the Polish competition, because mushrooms grew in real abundance there. Tentsmuir Forest borders on the beach and so if you are going there to enjoy mushrooming, take your basket, which you will certainly be able to fill full of mushrooms, and go all the way to the beach. You may be lucky enough to see seals frolicking in the sea.

We were surprised by another gift of nature. There were bramble bushes all around our part of Cumbernauld. Some grew right along the paths and some were in parks and fields. In early autumn the brambles were ripe, but no one seemed to be picking them. So we took a bucket and went out for them. On our way home the local children were curious and asked what it was we had. We gave each of them a handful to take home and show their parents. They came back quickly and said, "Mum says they're poisonous!" Nature could be too mysterious for some of those who had been transferred from an industrial city to the countryside.

However, the same people knew what to do when they heard the tunes of mobile shops. A van came to our street every day. These mobile shops would not be seen in the more affluent quarters; the people living there did their shopping by car in big shopping centres. The poor were made poorer by spending their change on fish and chips, hamburgers, sweets, ice cream, soft drinks, and so on. At first I was annoyed by it, but later just accepted it as their way of life. Two of our neighbours met at the fish and chip van every Thursday and went home with their supper saying, "Just for a wee change!"

Our two boys, Lukas and Benjamin, were drawn to the young driver of a sweetie van. The sweets in Scotland were different from Czech ones. The vendor noticed that our boys spoke in a funny language and he got a kick out of imitating the sounds. In return, our two echoed his Glaswegian sounds, which the man did not like at all. The teasing turned more serious when the boys started to knock on the van or they closed the back door when the man was in the front. Then he would throw things at them or splash them with whatever came into his hands. It was a kind of war that broke out between them. It culminated with Lukas and Benjamin imprisoning him in the van by sticking a nail in the door. When he got out, he gave them a proper chase. They escaped, but stopped bothering him. They probably realised that they had gone too far.

"This was the centre of our lives", I would think later, when I saw Balloch-Eastfield flash past the train to Edinburgh, where I used to go from Glasgow, when it became our new home, to attend meetings. The world which had been ours for almost five years seemed to have shrunk. But people we liked still lived their lives there.

Pastoral care is the same at home and in Scotland. Pastoral endeavour means entering into direct contact with people from all sorts of walks of life. Of course it was easier at home, although even there it was never straightforward. But the language and cultural barriers made my pastoral endeavour very challenging all the time I was in Scotland.

In Scotland, the first thing I realised was how ill prepared I was for constantly meeting new people. I had come from a rural congregation which was easily encompassed, and I very rarely came across a person I did not know or, at least, had not heard about. In Scotland, it was the exact opposite. For the whole time, eleven years, I was always seeing new faces, learning new names, opening new doors and following the lives of people I had never heard about before.

Pastoral care is the strength of the Church of Scotland. A visit by the minister is surprisingly appreciated, not only by members of the Church. I remember how in the first months I stood or sat in hospital beside the sick with a feeling of embarrassment that I did not know what to do or say. "Why am I here?" I would ask myself. Now, in retrospect, I see that I was given an opportunity to learn how to keep quiet. Am I able to be quiet now?

Once I asked a close colleague and friend of mine, John, about the position of a Church of Scotland minister in society. John was very critical of the Church, but his answer was unambiguous: "Yes, ministers of the Church of Scotland are recognised and trusted by both members of the Church and of society".

Another thing that surprised me in the first days was the openness of those I visited. It probably stemmed from the trust people felt towards a minister: a minister was soon a friend, a brother or a sister, a confessor. Before I came to understand it, I had a strange feeling that I was peeping into other people's kitchens and bedrooms and their dark corners. There were, of course, joys and visions that I was also allowed to share. Sometimes I would say to myself, "I wish I could understand better! I wish I could react more appropriately, in the right way!" I should add that what I am trying to describe here are my experiences with people in Glasgow.

I see our Czech environment as rather repressive in this respect. My experience in Prague is often of closed or even locked doors, closed and locked hearts. I sense that it shows the loneliness and hidden or unacknowledged anxiety of those who have got used to keeping to themselves too much.

In Scotland, there is usually a very lively communication between the minister, elders, members of the congregation and people 'outside'. It is expected that the minister will visit, listen, say something and give advice and, if possible, help and share whatever is on people's minds. Is that too much of a generalisation? Is the reality different? We can probably say yes and no.

Pictures from my pastoral visits in Scotland flicker through my mind and I feel again the pressure of human needs, confusion and misery, either others' or my own. However, I also relive the joy at the fact that I, a Czech, from a faraway place, different in many ways, was accepted with unreserved respect and love. It must have been the typical straightforwardness with which people in Glasgow approach others. I wish we, in the Czech Republic, were able to open ourselves towards one another and also towards the One who gives us life.

CHAPTER 17

LONELINESS, MEETING THE IONA COMMUNITY AND A LAST ENCOUNTER

These were our first summers in Scotland: the children at home in Czechoslovakia and the two of us behind the wall in Britain. Did it mean that we were homesick and in tears? Not exactly. We were curious about the new country. I remember how we tried to find 'variations on an existing theme'; experiences resembling what we had known and liked before we left home.

Summer work camps were the first thing that came to our minds, because it was there we found each other. Could we discover something similar in the British Isles? Our curiosity was raised by the abbreviation BTCV, 'British Trust for Conservation Volunteers' and we enrolled for one of their summer projects. Romantic yearning took us all the way to Falmouth in Cornwall.

What we found was somehow different from what we had expected. For example, everyone had to pay for taking part. Work was organised in a professional way. "If we make a lousy job of it, we won't get invited back," said Steve, our leader. He was from Cornwall and his grandmother had been a Cornish speaker.

We worked hard in a nature reserve where we built a wooden footpath round a lake surrounded by bushes and trees. There were plenty of anglers keen on catching fish. Their catch would be carp or bream which weighed a couple of pounds. For a fee the angler was allowed to catch, weigh, measure and take a photograph and then carefully put the fish back into the water. I just imagined the torn mouths of the fishes and so I could not get excited about their consideration.

The local ranger knew every fish by name; an enormous carp was George, just for an example. The ranger was very vigilant: to take a catch and have it for dinner? No way! Salmon, trout and other sea fish can be eaten. The ones in the lake were only for 'fishing the English way'! Our task was to construct an access path to the lake, because the ground was muddy and the natural path was getting wider and wider. We drove posts in with a heavy sledgehammer, and then we joined them with beams on which we fixed boards with nails. In the end, chicken wire was attached to the boards, so that the path would not be slippery. All this was done very carefully with the help of a spirit level. The spaces between the boards had to be regular, the posts had to be properly sharpened and driven in to the exact level. A job as perfect as possible!

Our Cornish leader was very observant and, especially at the beginning, he would check every post, measure every gap and tear off the boards that were not straight, murmuring something about a lousy job. What could he do with twelve people who came for a holiday from all corners of England and the two of us from Scotland? "Should we not mutiny against the severe supervision?" we thought. But he managed to keep us under control and the final result was a nice stretch of wooden footpath with boards evenly spaced.

It was hard work indeed and we were tired at the end of each day. With my forest work experience, I became the leader of one of the two teams and the 'chief rammer'.

I was fascinated by the variety of ways in which people handled tools, skillfully or otherwise. There was a puny young fellow from Oxford, just out of high school. I admired how he swung the sledgehammer and drove the posts in the most unyielding ground. But there were also others who were just not able to find the proper rhythm and swing. This brought to my mind my helpers in the Teleci forest. One was Hans, a well-built friend from Switzerland. He insisted on going to work with me. However, he could not hold an axe properly. Not one swing got finished: the impact of the axe was spoiled by his totally unnecessarily slowing it down before it fell. He spent twice as much energy and did not chop the branches off at the trunk; he just could not do the job . . .

Let us return to Cornwall though: how about leisure time at such an unusual work camp? It was our biggest problem: we worked as a team at the lake, but then, tiredness and lack of common motivation resulted in what was for us a strange isolation. After a frugal meal, almost like at our work camps back in our youth, everyone sought seclusion with their blisters and calluses, a book or a beer. Daniela and I read or talked together and remembered how different our work camps back home used to be with all the discussions and games. The physical conditions at the British project were comparable to our camps, but we missed the sense of community.

Self-pity shackles creativity. It does not look around. It does not expect anything. It does not dream. Or if it does dream, it looks back at the dreams of the past. And self pity prevents us from realising what we are doing. How can we open our eyes when we want to keep them shut? How can we listen attentively when we don't want to hear? How can we find friends and kindred spirits when we close the door?

However it may still happen that all of a sudden we will look and see. We will listen and hear and we will feel moved to open a closed door at least a little. Or is somebody else trying to open it for us?

In 1987 we received an invitation to attend a conference at Swanwick in Derbyshire. Swanwick is a village where there is a conference centre. The conference was called 'Church on Fire' and Daniela and I were invited to say something about ourselves, who we were and where we came from. People from different parts of the world were to consider the response of the Christian Church in places where there were flames of tension and conflict. The divided Europe was one of them.

I told the delegates about the many walls in Britain. There were walls everywhere. They mostly marked out the boundaries of fields for cattle and sheep. When you went for a walk in the open countryside, you had to climb over them. There was still a Wall in Berlin at that time. Its purpose was totally to separate East from West. However, the West was afflicted by it too as its eastern neighbour had been severed from it. Separated by Walls, Europeans must have noticed that they were thought of as cattle and sheep.

The British participants were disturbed by the image of walls in their country. But in what other way could the absurdity of a Europe rent asunder be made plain? The German delegates accepted my illustration with gratitude. We agreed that 'their' Wall crippled all Europeans.

How did all this lead us to Iona? Imagine a conference with a hundred participants. Some of them were there to share something of the discord and conflict in their societies. That was certainly enough to make the programme and atmosphere compelling.

However, at a Christian conference there is usually also a chaplain who is in charge of worship.

A group of three Scots from Glasgow, members of the 'Wild Goose Worship Group', had been invited to lead the worship during the conference. We had to travel from Scotland to England to meet Christine, Graham and John. They shared in the programme by leading morning, evening and Sunday worship and by being open to informal pastoral conversations. Their part in the conference became the highlight because of their simple and appropriate liturgies and new songs. They invited others to participate. In their talks to the children there was movement and action, which was unusual for us.

Now, I can see a lot of new ideas at home too and I am very glad. But then we were parched and stiff from being different and isolated. And there, at the Sunday service, children came to us and whispered their secrets in our ears: Jesus was homeless, Jesus was not white, he did not speak English and, in fact, he did not have a father. And immediately after that we sang a song which celebrated the Father of all, the Lord of lords and our Saviour. And then we heard, as if anew, about the Iona Community, about the island of Iona in the Atlantic in the Inner Hebrides with its Abbey, about family groups and their concern for the poor and the developing world.

No, I was not blindly enthused. I knew that the members of the Iona Community came mostly from the background of intellectuals, intelligentsia and middle class; a friend and minister in a deprived area in Glasgow explained that to me. It is, of course, a crucial problem. How to grasp poverty at the grassroots? How to share it and not be condescending?

I see a picture of Leo Tolstoy and his attempts to get close to the poor 'muzhiks'. Dressed as a poor man he ate buckwheat meal. What he did not know was that those around him had always secretly enhanced it.

However, the Iona Community helped us to open our eyes, ears and hearts again and to complete our entry into Scotland.

It was while I was at Condorrat that I had my last and perhaps saddest encounter with my old foe, Milan Opocensky, whom I had last seen driving past the manse in Teleci without daring to speak to me. Now in post as General Secretary of the World Alliance of Reformed Churches, Opocensky was invited to a week of meetings in Scotland. His wish was to meet Scottish colleagues and so a visit was arranged to a Presbytery meeting. It happened to be the Presbytery of Falkirk, of which I was a member.

I heard that the General Secretary of the World Alliance of Reformed Churches, Dr Milan Opocensky, was to address the Presbytery. My first reaction was to stay at home. On second thoughts I said to myself, "Is it the case even in Scotland that I can't go where I want to go and where I belong? Nobody in Scotland has ever banned me from a church meeting as used to happen at home."

And so I sat in the church of Falkirk High and the Moderator moved that the General Secretary of the Alliance of Reformed Churches, Dr Milan Opocensky, would like to address the Presbytery. All the people present, except one who was against, agreed. Milan conveyed greetings and described the difficult situation of the churches in Eastern Europe, namely in Czechoslovakia. He was grateful to the Church of Scotland that he could tell them about the plight of brothers and sisters in his home church, and he added, ". . . for there is one of the afflicted ones sitting here among you, sent by our church, my dear brother Tomas Bisek."

During the interval, Milan saw me and hurried with open arms in my direction. I put up my hand in refusal and said, "It's not possible." Milan said, "Now here, let's forgive one another!" We never met again.

It torments me how I have somehow let that relationship slip, be blown away. Did I have no responsibility towards someone who probably never stopped doubting that he and I belonged to the same community of God's people? Did he speak about forgiveness in a way that was too hasty and easy? Did it not have any basis? Was it not clear enough what we should say sorry for? And did his request not contain his hope of reconciliation? Is my hope different? Am I not at fault if I don't try hard enough to see how it was the hostile regime that had divided us?

For the first five years, until November 1989, Daniela and I wrote home regularly. Especially for us, the two adults, correspondence was hopefully an encouragement that perhaps one day . . .

The last letter from the time of forced separation and yearning is dated August 1989:

Dear Middle-Europeans,

We are in Whitby and our old caravanette is sitting, sunbathing on an embankment above the North Sea. It is good to enjoy the sunshine. Rain will often get us soaked. May we enjoy the sun while it is shining.

From the van we see the expanse of steel-blue sea. There are fishing boats and freighters rocking on the waves. It is too early to spot any sailing boats. At eleven in the morning, summer time, the road along the embankment is slowly getting busy with cars, and people in summer clothes are going down the green paths to the sea. Some are taking the 'Cliff Lift'.

The beach below us looks welcoming. But Daniela will first finish a chapter of her book *The Small Woman*, about a missionary in China, and I will write a few lines for you distant ones.

We are looking forward to walking through the town. Its history has made it attractive. The old ruined abbey bears witness to that. Whitby was attacked by the Vikings several times. It was ravaged by Henry VIII and, finally, the Germans bombed it during World War One.

We have read about the explorations of Captain James Cook, who sailed all the way to Antarctica. We are interested in the whaling tradition which is presented in the local museum and also recognisable in the town.

We invite you for a walk with us. You will get energy from a kipper smoked on oak which we are going to buy for you. Then we will set out along the river Esk and enjoy all that the banks of the river and the sea offer us.

Wait a minute, please, though. I need to sort out my whirling thoughts regarding our old problem: our arrival in Great Britain.

Now and then we hear a critical word about allowing our children to grow up in the constant, unsettling movement between Scotland and Czechoslovakia. "You are making it even more difficult for them. Their visits home make the past seem ideal to them. They should settle down in the new world and get rooted, make friends and live where you have to be."

I wish we were able to accept it when others try to feel for our difficulties entering a new world, a new language, a new culture. And still, I think that there is more to it.

First of all, the critical comments come because the children do keep going back home. If we limited our whole existence only to Scotland, there would be nothing to say. There would simply be no opportunity. And we would all integrate and settle fast into the new environment.

However, my question is: should it be like this? Is speed something that is desired? Is it good to suppress the past? Is it necessary? Is it a guarantee of a fuller life?

And there is also another thing: how come that we are here? How did we get so far from home? Why are we here? How did it come to this? And why should we want to deprive our children of the Czech-ness into which they were born and which they desire? Why should we force Scottish-ness on them if they feel it is alien? Why should it be that way? Why should the consideration of those with experience prevail, even if parents are among them?

I still remember the pressure of the authorities and the police which had been going on for years before our emigration. There was anxiety and most of all frustration caused by the constant disturbance of the normal flow of things; there were summonses, questionings and threats. I still remember the struggle after I had found the bugging system in our manse, when my license to work as a minister was revoked for incompetence which was not specified. There was the ridiculous "A spy is working in the forest", conveyed to me by a local Party member who had returned from a regional Party meeting. It was necessary for the State Security to take my finger- and palm-prints (probably in case I lost them while working with a chainsaw – how providential!). I remember how I refused to accept that my calling to ministry should end with my license and be limited by the national boundary.

So the two of us have become 'prisoners of the border line' and we are trying to find a new beginning.

However, there is an insistent question: is it possible to minister without borders? Is there a life outwith the border line, a life on the other side? This is probably one of the crucial questions for an immigrant. We meet Czech expatriates who have relinquished their roots. They deny them, they conceal them, they get angry and alienated, and they suffer. They do not want to bear the wounds. They are like sick people, who are disabled and therefore do not want to accept the reality of their handicap. At the same time, this strange disability is blatant as the constant, unsuccessful denial of the real state of affairs is blatant. What is emigration then? Is it a disease?

I would think it is. The struggle to bear it is a crucial effort. It is, in a way, a struggle for life. I do not have in mind only the emigration of taking our possessions to the other end of the world like Jonah. I also mean inner emigration. There are many who go into 'emigration' at home; they emigrate into their privacy, their weekend cottage, their car, their worries and frustrations, their unhappiness or assumed happiness.

There is probably also the emigration of a whole nation, when people lose sight of the journey they are on and take their eyes off the Word which gives courage to acknowledge the truth and deny the lie.

I will get back to our 'entering' the new world, the beginning of our sickness. And I have a question: Is it possible for a person to say that he or she was not born where they were born or did not live where they lived? Should we not rather listen to the invitation to be sojourners, guests who fill their days by living from what they have been and trying to remember what they should or could become?

In a world of mobility and change the longing for the final destination is great. It manifests itself so that even as a guest I want truth and peace for others, for the world and for myself.

What is the journey home? Where does it lead? Yes, there certainly is home. We belong somewhere now, already, as wanderers. That is our earthly place. In spite of that, however, we can, all together, find peace and a Home above all homes.

So, will you join us now and go down to the sun-drenched beach, then on into town and make a short expedition with Captain Cook to find the sixth continent?

Yours, Tomas

Chapter 18

PARISH MINISTRY IN GLASGOW

Until November 1989 I was an associate minister in Condorrat Parish Church. During those four years and more I learned a great deal from my Scottish colleague. I also had the chance to see what it meant to be the second minister and, at the same time, equal to a colleague who was 'the first'. We can ask an investigative question: you were the second and you were equal? Or, were you equally the second? My answer would be that I was simply the second; that was it. It was my simply first colleague who decided our mutual business and congregational affairs. Sometimes it was a relief for me and sometimes it was a little the other way.

An associate minister is usually called for five years. Then there is an appraisal and the call can be extended for another five years. The year 1989 was my fifth year as an associate. It was also the year of all the dramas of the crumbling totalitarian regimes in Eastern Europe. All of a sudden, we had to consider what to do next. We had not expected such a complicated and, at the same time, joyous situation.

In those more than four years we had probably gradually integrated into the Scottish environment. Becoming distanced from our homeland was almost inevitable. This was confirmed by the Central Offices of the Church of Scotland when they invited me for an interview at the end of the fourth year. The secretary spoke openly, "You are not as young as you were. And you probably don't reckon you could return home. So you don't have to be an associate minister permanently. You may face difficulties when looking for an independent charge. It means that you will have to send in applications. People in the congregations are unpredictable; they have their vision of an ideal minister. He should be a graduate from a well-known university, he should be friendly, he should be middle-aged, have a wife and two children, should have an interesting hobby, should be experienced . . . and he should be a Scot. We cannot give directives to the congregations. I suggest that you throw your net wide. Don't be afraid of the North. It is better to be farther from the Central Belt and on your own rather than a permanent associate, don't you think?"

Before leaving Teleci, when the Charter 77 hunt was at its fiercest, we had received a card from Scotland. It came from the Atlantic, the Daliburgh manse in South Uist. The manse family was part of a group who supported people in Eastern Europe. They had written to us, unknown folk in Teleci, and told us how they collected drift wood from the sea to burn in their stoves. We looked Daliburgh up in our atlas and dreamed romantically of peace on the shores of the stormy ocean.

Later in Scotland, I attended meetings of the World Mission and Unity Board at '121' in Edinburgh. I met the Revd Gavin Elliott, who was a member of the Africa Committee. He had spent six years in Zambia. After returning from Africa, he became minister of the South Uist Parish and so he and his family lived in the Daliburgh manse. Yes, it was 'our' Daliburgh! The founder of the Iona Community, George MacLeod, spoke in this way about coincidences: "If you think that this is a coincidence, I wish you a very dull life!"

Gavin had no idea that his predecessors had expressed solidarity with us, but he was of agile mind and immediately acted in a very friendly way. Without wasting time he invited the Czech minister of the Church of Scotland to preach in Daliburgh. He chose the Communion Season, which was the climax in the Hebridean church year. I still feel very pleased that I preached in 'our' Daliburgh and rejoiced with the congregation round the Table of Christ's forgiveness. With some regret I remember that despite a lot of teasing Gavin did not allow me to preach in Czech, although he preached one of his preparatory sermons in Gaelic. Yes, he managed to do it after six months of preparation. Then he said: "And never again! I was not sure what I was saying."

"And I am supposed to be sure what I am saying in my English!" I thought.

I went to the Hebrides with Daniela and our eldest daughter, Lucie. The beautiful, but often wet and stormy islands offered us lovely September weather. Gavin took us out to sea in his little boat.

"I'll be steering the boat and you fish," Gavin said.

"Us? How?" we asked.

"Here are lines with feathers and hooks. Just throw them in and keep pulling gently at them," Gavin instructed us.

We were sorry that our youngest, Benjamin, was not with us. He would have known how to keep pulling gently. We tried our best to follow the instructions of a specialist, Lucie and I to no avail, but Daniela always felt something, then gave it a proper pull and in a little while a beautiful fish was swinging on the hook. She pulled out seven fishes. What kind? There were six mackerel and one saithe, all of them at least ten inches long. After her third fish, I changed lines with her, to try the magic. It didn't work for me! She kept pulling mackerel out of the sea even with my line. Gavin was amused at the faces I made.

However, as you can see, Daliburgh never became our congregation. Another possible place I had haphazardly noted, when still in Teleci, was the picturesque town of Pitlochry. It was only a random choice, to comfort us that there was a place we could go to and that we would not end up in limbo. I remember that in Teleci we would say: "Under no circumstances would we go to a city!" and Glasgow seemed to be the most forbidding with all the industry and crisis, fog and desolation. In Cumbernauld, too, we kept saying that Glasgow was not an option for us. It was especially our children, who felt Glasgow to be a symbol of humiliation and suffering when we first arrived and they went to language school there. They did not know or understand anything then. So they just said, "Choose any place, but not Glasgow!" However a year before I succeeded in the hunt for a vacant charge, Lucie finished high school and was looking for a place at university. She wanted to stay in Scotland and was offered places in Edinburgh and Glasgow. She went to see both universities and decided that Glasgow was better. "Why can't we move to Glasgow?" she suggested.

So I made copies of my curriculum vitae and started to look for vacancies. The process reminded me of the procedure back home before leaving for Scotland when I tried to find a congregation for which I would be given a licence. There the government authorities, advised by the State Security, were always an immovable obstacle. The Scottish experience was, of course, different, because I 'fought' the congregations or, rather, the vacancy committees. I think that I applied to about ten congregations that in the end did not want me. Then I applied to Govanhill in Glasgow.

But that was not a straightforward process either. After several meetings with the vacancy committee and preaching as sole nominee, I finally signed a statement that I had not brought influence to bear on anybody, nor had I been influenced by anybody. The Church of Scotland is very cautious in this respect, probably as a result of experience. I wish the procedure for filling vacancies in our Czech

Church congregations was similarly independent of recommendations: they rely too much on who knows whom and who is related to whom. It always disturbs me.

In the end, at the beginning of November 1989, I was elected minister of Govanhill Trinity Church. Was that a coincidence? I accepted it gratefully. I still wonder at the fact that only two weeks later the Velvet Revolution in Czechoslovakia quite unexpectedly opened up new possibilities for us, which made us think again about what to do. Our forced emigration was over. Should we not go home?

The interim Moderator and Glasgow Presbytery guessed what state of mind I was in and they gave me the possibility not to accept the charge. But I could not. I could not decline an invitation confirmed by an election. I remember the precautionary question of the interim Moderator: "Will you stay for at least five years?" I answered simply, "Yes, I'll do my best."

We stayed in Govanhill for nearly six years. What were they like?

The largest, once the most industrialized and now still the most Scottish of cities did not give us an impression of a clean place. It was sliced in two by a motorway, deformed by right-angled high-rise flats

GOVANHILL TRINITY CHURCH

140

and empty expanses after demolitions. But you could also find lovely spots there. We, however, saw Edinburgh as a beauty among cities. How could Glasgow compete?

We still remember how Glaswegians made fun of Edinburgh because they could not do anything about its primacy. For example: "There is more fun at a funeral in Glasgow than at a wedding in Edinburgh." Or, "The best thing in Edinburgh is the train going to Glasgow."

What arguments! They are the words of those who used to work in the dockyards, steelworks, mines, chemical or textile industries. In the past, a proper Glaswegian had just left the factory or the pub. He was on the way to a football match or was trying to find his way home. He worked with his hands and used his head to ease his plight, to say a pert word, to sneer or mock, and to sing. And when Glaswegians sang, it must have been the Irish in them, who had been brought to Glasgow by dire poverty and hopelessness. They had accepted their plight long ago, they sang and joked. I am sure you would enjoy listening to them. You would feel empathy and joy.

Those who were on the margins of society, and there were lots of them in Glasgow, helped themselves with a particular openness. It was possible to say that their poverty was open. They were expectant, they did not pretend good standing, they did not have time to fuss and yet they liked to play . . . openness is a challenge and it took me a good while to get used to it.

In Glasgow, I tried gingerly to find the inner potential of the beatitude of poverty. People were at the mercy of circumstances. They felt inadequate and anxious because of their awareness of being weak. I accept Jesus' promise to those who struggle because, though they are not ready or able, they are still somehow open to the people they meet and to whatever comes their way. I don't think that it is so easy to approach those who have enough and who know that they are in good standing. And it is difficult to see in them the urgent challenge of belonging to others.

A question is puzzling my mind: why were Glaswegians special to me? And I would also turn the question round: what did they see in us? Yes, why did they take us in; why did they accept and respect us? I remember how we took our bikes to look around Glasgow. After a while, in a small park, we took out a map and tried to see where we were and where to go next. In a moment another cyclist stopped and wanted to help. Oh, in fact, he would go with us and show us the way . . . he did not wait for us to agree. He led the way and kept talking.

After a while he stopped and we tried to apologise for taking him out of his way. "It's O.K.", he said and continued, "In fact, it's not O.K.". It was his first ride after heart surgery. His wife had let him go just for a little while and there he was, showing off with us despite not feeling very well . . . and off he went. We still belong to Glasgow and some Glaswegians still belong to us.

Yes, we had a home in Glasgow, but we did not have the feeling of owning anything. It is usually so in a manse. And fortunately so! Otherwise, as rules and regulations sometimes get interpreted in a variety of ways, the Church might end up without manses. We felt settled and accepted in Glasgow. It was very special to have a place in a foreign country and feel somehow 'at home'. I am glad we could have the experience.

The unassuming spontaneity of the fellowship of the congregation in Govanhill had an immediate effect. I had a very pleasing feeling that a Glaswegian would not let me feel out of place and live as an outsider. People around us did not take into account the trauma that pressed on us. They were interested in other things. But they acknowledged our coming there and being with them. That was it. They did not fuss over us and they spoke to us as to those who belonged among them in all respects.

We all know that during Advent we hear carols not only at home but also in the shops. They help to create the special atmosphere of the season. It was a little different in our church in Czechoslovakia. There we do not talk about carols but about Christmas hymns or church hymns although the two, folk and liturgical, blend.

In Scotland the church has 'lent' its Christmas carols to the secular world. It took our family a while to get used to church carols being played in the supermarket. We did not like it. We sang the same carols in church on Sunday. You can have too much of a good thing!

The congregation sang with gusto at Sunday services. The Scots like to sing familiar Christmas carols enthusiastically as if they had not been sung in shops many times during the week. It was like with little children who always want the same thing. Change is not acceptable.

It was at Advent that I got a slap in the face. Let me say first that I have thought quite a lot about liturgy and singing, especially at Advent and Christmas. It was perhaps because the Scottish Christmas carols were different from the ones we used to sing at home. On the other hand, being back in the Czech Republic now, I fondly remember the Scottish Advent singing in Govanhill.

And the 'slap'? It was caused by the hymn "Once in royal David's city" which was composed in Victorian times. In the Church Hymnary third edition the words describe the baby and the boy Jesus as a very good and obedient child. Therefore all Christian children must be good as Jesus was and they will become stars in white around him in heaven.

We were delighted to find a paraphrase *Once in Judah's least-known city* from the workshop of John Bell and Graham Maule. The melody was the same but the words were grounded in realism.

It was a very interesting discovery for both Daniela and me. Then Eve whispered to Adam, "Take a bite" and Daniela whispered to me, "Make copies for the church, so that we can sing it at Christmas". I was very happy to follow this advice. The result was a sheet with two songs, one on each page. The original song was for the first Sunday. Some people, of course, read the words of the *Once in Judah's least-known city* in advance and were horrified.

I was hauled over the coals at the next meeting of the Kirk Session. "You think we're going to sing this?" I was asked, and I realised that the group, which was normally divided, had formed one unit. We had defiled a hymn! We had trampled the gentle poetry! We had recklessly touched a soft spot . . . to defend myself I read from the Gospels of Matthew and Luke and tried to point out the critical moments. No, such a brutal text cannot be sung! Then, in despair, I pointed out that the Church of Scotland maintained that the liturgy and order of service are the responsibility of the minister alone. That was the end of the matter.

However, not completely – for at the end of the meeting an elder, one of my closest, Helen, asked, "We haven't said how it will be on Sunday. Are we going to sing it?"

I had to say what was inevitable, "No, we aren't".

"But we haven't voted! Who decided?" Helen asked.

"I did," was my reply.

"But you wanted to sing it, didn't you?" she asked again.

"That's true. But I can sing it at home if nobody here wants to join me". I finished the discussion and felt as if I had won a battle – but, of course, I had lost a war.

It is said that Glasgow, in fact, comprises a number of villages, which makes the city more humane, I think. Yes, a majority of the people have come from the country and in some ways their relationships are like those in a tightly knit community. It is natural for them to see others and listen and speak to them. Surely, they also have their conflicts, but they do not ignore one another.

Despite having moved to the city we were also able to continue our mushroom-gathering exploits. I conducted a funeral service for the husband of a member of the Govanhill Trinity congregation, Mrs Muriel Bernardon. She told me how her deceased Italian husband had enjoyed looking for new spots where there were lots of mushrooms and keeping them secret, as he had done in his homeland. Their son David, a keen car mechanic, wanted us to know about his father's mushrooming places and 'keep them safe'. He said that he did not have time for mushroom hunting. On a prearranged day he took us south of Glasgow and there we combed a beech wood and the fertile grassy edges of a track, he for the last time and we for the first. The harvest was respectable. When we met at his car again, David wrung his hands and said, "All your mushrooms are poisonous! They're turning blue!" – "Ours? Poisonous?" I replied and wanted to tell him that all his mushrooms were poisonous and that he should throw them away. I thought, why was it that we seemed to be picking different mushrooms and then I said, "Of course for centuries you, Italians, have got used to the poison of these mushrooms. Our resistance is different. If we exchanged our collections, we would all come to a bad end!"

The poverty of many of Glasgow's residents came home to me again at a funeral I took not long after my arrival in Govanhill. The funeral Directors phoned, "A Mr James Macdonald has died. Will you take the funeral service?"

I asked, "Do you know anything about him?"

"No, we don't. He did not have any family. He was on his own," was the answer.

"How come?" I asked.

"He was homeless."

"What about friends or colleagues?" I asked.

"No one seems to have known him. We don't know if there are any distant relatives. Will you take the service?"

"Of course, when will it take place?" I asked.

"At the Linn cemetery tomorrow at eleven. The gravedigger will show you where the grave is."

"I will be there," I said and added, "If you get any more information, let me know, please."

"Of course."

I cycled to the cemetery the next day. No more information had come. I thought about human dignity, how transitory a person was and about the pain God must feel when someone from His family has passed away, utterly alone. I parked the bicycle and went to the freshly dug grave and waited. It was eleven o'clock. Then I saw a black hearse on the road. It stopped and two men in black got out of the vehicle. They brought a coffin to the grave, put it on the stands and turned to me saying, "It's terrible, Minister. What shall we do? There's no-one here. What shall we do?"

"How do you mean no-one is here?" I asked and said, "I can see three people here." The gravedigger was also there in addition to the two funeral attendants.

"But there's no one except us! How can we do the burial if no one is here?" they went on. I repeated again that there were four of us, enough to say a prayer and perform the burial ceremony. "Really?" one of the funeral attendants said in disbelief. I opened my Bible and read out a consoling Word before saying a prayer . . .

The burial was over. One of the funeral attendants approached me and thanked me emotionally, as if he were a close relative of the deceased.

Two members of the Govanhill Trinity Church lived across the street from the manse. They were the first ones we visited after moving in. The man was a retired policeman. He let us know what being a policeman meant by saying: "Listen, do you know that Glasgow is a smoke-free city? You are not to burn anything else than smokeless coal . . . Are you saying you'd like to burn wood from the garden? That shouldn't even cross your mind. Somebody will report you and you'll be in trouble."

There was an open fire in the manse – a luxury about which we only dreamt when we lived in Teleci, our first manse in the Bohemian Uplands, where we had more wood than we could ever burn. "But who would want to report us in Govanhill?" we asked ourselves and had an immediate answer: it must be our neighbour. He must have seen the smoke belching from our chimney and so he came over to put things right. It was hardly possible for us to comply with the warning. We knew that even our friends from the Iona Community found it difficult. They enjoyed sitting in front of their fires where twigs from the local parks or their gardens were burning.

This retired policeman was one of the few men on the church cleaning rota. They would join a group of women every Thursday morning to prepare the church for the Sunday service. The men were also regular and enthusiastic players of bowls either in the church hall in winter or on the green in summer. Our neighbour was also an active member of the Congregational Board. When he was not quite sixty years old he suffered from a serious heart condition and I remember seeing him in the Royal Infirmary after a heart operation. The surgeon had made him promise to stop smoking his pipe. The man said, "I'm not sure if I can manage." The surgeon replied, "It's your problem and, after all, it's your heart. I just need your promise." The promise was kept.

His wife was full of life, vivacious and indomitable. She knew everybody and everything about Govanhill. I can still hear her enthusiastic greetings shouted from a distance and then her sarcastic remarks and quips directed at us. Through her we had news about the Govanhill folk because she told us about anyone she had happened to meet. She showed genuine affection towards the old ladies in the church. They were all her friends. Once I dropped in unannounced and heard her raucous laughter at a 'hen party' she was holding in her living room. I was told that as the minister I was obliged not to see that about fifteen ladies were enjoying a raffle. No, gambling was not allowed in the Church of Scotland; not even for the church funds.

Our church treasurer's image comes from various church meetings. I can still see her waving a chocolate bar at an AGM meeting saying, "If you deny yourselves a Mars bar or a banana once a week, we'll be eight hundred pounds better off. And that is exactly what we need. Listen, I know that what people give in the offering envelopes is confidential but I do know who gives what!!!" Oh, I was mortified and I told her, "You mustn't do this. You're the church's treasurer." Her response was very innocent, "Just wait and see how effective it will be."

Another time, she was sitting next to me at the top table. Suddenly she turned to me saying, "Do you have to eat garlic before a meeting?" I was dumbfounded. What could I say? I just tried to remember what we had for dinner. Leaving the church that evening, she took my arm and said, "You're my lumber." And turning to the others, "Tomas is my lumber."

Like most of the church members, our treasurer was also a widow. Her husband had died after only a few years of marriage. Therefore she was permanently among her friends from the church. She enjoyed the routine after the Sunday service when she and those on the rota would sit in the Session room, count the money and smoke. Was smoking in the church building something one should not do? We never discussed it. I don't smoke. But what does it matter? Who would have remained in our churches if we chased the smokers away? They were the common Glasgow folk just as we were ordinary Czech folk. Times have changed since then. Smoking is not allowed in public places in Scotland now.

Govanhill Trinity Church had two session clerks because the congregation had been made up of a union between Govanhill Church and Candlish-Polmadie Church. The arrangement was that the session clerks of both congregations would continue to hold their offices. They got along very well. Without much discussion they easily decided what their responsibilities would be. They were both retired, both of the old school, which was the case for the majority of the congregation anyway.

One of the session clerks lived in Govanhill, the other one in East Kilbride, where he had moved a long time before, being given a house from his employer. He settled in a church in East Kilbride. After some time, my predecessor asked him whether he would like to return to the Govanhill congregation because they needed Sunday school teachers. That was it. He accepted the invitation and stayed for several more decades, not only as a Sunday school teacher but also as session clerk. He was a very amiable person, ready to talk to anyone. He made sure that everybody was made welcome. He loved talking to the children and always repeated how Jesus loved them. He used to say it so vehemently that I felt rather uneasy about his piety. I asked myself, "Wouldn't it put them off?" But those who met him must have felt his warm-hearted personality and the sincerity in his welcome. This was also what we, as a family, felt right from the beginning. During those more than six years in Govanhill Trinity Church I saw him growing old and frail. But his warm-heartedness and dedication to the church never diminished. He loved the church and the ministers more than anything. Therefore he was willing to travel from East Kilbride several times a week to be with us in Govanhill.

The originally Candlish-Polmadie Session clerk was always in the company of his wife and his sister-in-law. He was a witty person, probably from a slightly better-off background than most of other Govanhill folk. He was a caring husband in a childless marriage and a considerate brother-in-law to the handicapped sister of his wife. They were a constant 'triplet'. He had a small job in the office at Hampden

Park Stadium. Once he gave us two tickets for the game of Scotland against Poland. Our Ben and I went to our first official and, moreover, international football match. To our annoyance we managed to miss the only goal the Scots scored, because we were too busy watching the Scottish fans and did not see what was happening on the field. I remember saying, "Bother, we're not watching TV. We won't get a rerun in the stadium." All the time Ben kept telling me to be quiet. I asked, "Why? It is natural to speak up at a football match." He said, "If we speak aloud, the Scots will beat us up thinking we are Polish."

Another reality we became aware of in Glasgow was the large Pakistani community among whom we lived. How can a distant Asian country, albeit in miniature, sneak into reflections about Scotland? Visit Govanhill and take a walk along Allison Street on a weekday. You will see what I mean: stalls and tables with fruit and vegetables stand in front of the shop windows, or lean against the walls and railings of the usual three-storey sandstone buildings. The goods clutter up a big part of the pavements. The shop-owners have to argue with the police for space. The colourful and attractive-looking fruit and vegetables entice shoppers of all kinds. The shop-keepers' employees and families mingle with them.

The goods the Pakistanis in Glasgow sold were cheap and even the cheapest. It was obvious that they profited not from the price but from quantity. We never felt that we should shop anywhere else. I was fascinated by the Pakistanis' competition with one another. As if they did not notice; or was it something natural for them?

Just take a walk and you will feel that perhaps the whole of Govanhill, which is 'my' whole former parish, is almost totally Pakistani. It is the result of the different lifestyles of the two biggest groups that live there: the Pakistanis are used to living outside, on the street. The Scots spend most of their time indoors. One does not see them in the street.

In Albert Road, where we lived, there was a Pakistani family in the next-door house. Our back gardens shared a fence. I remember that shortly after we had moved in we were all in our gardens. I listened to the two languages: Urdu and Czech and said to myself, "So this is Glasgow!"

How did the Pakistanis get to Glasgow? There was a lot of work in Britain after the war. Menial jobs were offered to people from some of the former colonial countries. The opportunity to emigrate to Britain must have been rather attractive and so the result was that groups and individuals from Asian, African and Caribbean countries were scattered around Great Britain.

The second generation of these immigrants had grown up and they showed a certain trait of assimilation and conscious Britishness. I used to get my paper from a corner shop. The shop-keeper was an older Pakistani man, father of four. He was an ex-serviceman of the Pakistani Army and had lived in a small village in Pakistan. Then in Glasgow he dedicated his life to the newsagent's shop. He was full of memories of his homeland, to which he was not going to return. His four children had graduated from British universities and displayed the civic and political mindedness of coloured Britons. They knew their rights and responsibilities and were ready to promote and fulfil them.

How does the Pakistani presence in Scotland manifest itself? First, I want to say that some members of our congregation complained that, in comparison with their Pakistani neighbours, their financial and material situation was like second-class citizens. Sometimes I reacted to their complaints as I felt fit: I would say, "Open a greengrocer's shop and stay there every day from morning to evening. In a few years you will have the chance to get a BMW and a villa with a garden".

Of course, objecting to Pakistanis reflected a deeper dimension of the coexistence of the two communities. The majority of Pakistanis observed the Muslim faith and lifestyle. Life in a foreign country made them be clear and circumspect so as not to lose face. Thus the relationship of Scottish and Pakistani communities could be compared to fish living at different depths; living next to one another and, at the same time, not intermingling. Our congregation was, with no exception, white and almost completely Scottish. I was troubled by it.

Now, after the lapse of time, I understand that families with quite different lifestyles can live next to each other in a friendly and even creative relationship; they do not trouble one another. It manifests itself in silent albeit unstable tolerance.

It seems to me that we really see the whole family of mankind 'as a reflection in a mirror' and we don't understand much of it. For example, when we are faced with a different form of Christian piety, it is enough to irk us. May we open ourselves with the determination of our ancestors from Jan Amos Comenius' time: let us live side by side as parts of a whole which manifests diversity and together let us form the family of man. May we be willing to stand by one another, support one another and help those who are different.

Chapter 19

RETURNING HOME

The disintegration of the totalitarian regime in Czechoslovakia was an extremely joyful event for us. Even so, it wasn't easy to leave Scotland after we had overcome so many obstacles that had stood in our way as we tried to settle in such a new world. Our thinking about returning to the Czech Republic was made a little easier for us by the promise we had made when leaving for Scotland that we would go back if the door were opened. However, as I had been called to be elected parish minister of Govanhill in Glasgow just at the time of the changes in the Eastern Bloc, it would be nearly seven years before we returned home.

This delay made it possible for us to begin to rebuild severed ties and establish new contacts while also giving us time to try to imagine how to start. A helpful factor was that I had been a regular contributor to the religious broadcasts of the Czech Section of the BBC World Service for several years before the Velvet Revolution. The recordings were made in Glasgow, at the BBC Studios in Queen Margaret Drive, and were then sent by post to London to be broadcast to Czechoslovakia. When I was in Prague in January 1990, for the first time after the regime had changed, I visited the Theological Seminary and noticed a small poster on the board: 'Bisek preaches on the BBC tomorrow at 4.15.' I rejoiced. They knew about me!

The door to returning home from Scotland was opened for us by the kind invitation of the Ministers' Union of our Church. They asked me to give a talk at their annual conference in February 1991. I was to talk about the Church from which I had been separated for seven years. The theme I was given, "The Identity of the Evangelical Church of Czech Brethren", gave me the opportunity not only to examine our Czech Protestant church but also to try to understand some of the differences between the two churches in which I had served as a minister. When the talks were published in a church magazine, the title was *Czech Protestantism and Scotland* and the headings of individual talks were: 'How was the first church formed?', 'What does it mean to be together?', 'Some Remarks on the origins of the Evangelical Church of Czech Brethren', 'The Legacy of the past', 'Carrying each other's burdens', 'Spreading the living Word', 'Life in community' and 'The Fellowship of pilgrims'. I spoke about my understanding of ecclesiology and focused especially on the crisis in the Evangelical Church of Czech Brethren whose full extent had been revealed in the new era. I knew I had to speak very openly.

The response to my presentation was generally positive although somebody voiced a reproach that while living away from the Church I had no right to talk about it. In the lively discussion that followed, somebody said clearly that there was no point in listening to 'someone who hasn't been living here'. What I had anticipated was confirmed: 'It's either a saviour or a traitor who comes from the free world.'

Someone else added that it was strange that I had left the country as an adversary of socialism and came back as its supporter. Should I have understood that I had not been seen as being critical of the totalitarian government but of its socialist ideals? Of course, this was the beginning of the church's existence in a new situation which was extremely turbulent and quickly changing; to a certain extent we became part of the domestic discussion within the Czech church, although we had not yet settled into our future home. Living in Scotland for some years, I was influenced by Scottish society, which is itself influenced by principles of social solidarity. I also accepted the challenge of the Iona Community, whose main concern is spiritual renewal expressed through solidarity with the poor, excluded and marginalised. I know I make my friends at home sound more critical than they really were, for in spite of various differences of opinion the arms of many were open wide.

After this experience it was a pleasure to be thinking of the possibility of returning home. Invitations from several vacant congregations were encouraging. It was surprising for some that we declined to consider a congregation near Teleci, my first charge, from where we had been forced into exile. Some people imagined that our return to the area would crown our victorious venture. Had we become Local Heroes? This notion had indeed developed after we had left in 1985, when the State Security were no longer present in the village and its surrounding area. Our 'heroism' did not endanger anyone any more. Then, when emotions and excitement were running high after the change, Teleci had someone to be celebrated. Since of course we were hundreds of miles away, such a hero or prophet didn't put anyone at risk.

Our close friends in the church in Teleci, and also some others, thought that we would return to the place where we had lived with them and from which we had been banished. But it wasn't possible. We recognised that that would not be an option. How would I carry out my ministerial duties in an atmosphere of such unbalanced adulation? "No one is good but God alone . . ." (Mark 10:18)

There was a myth that "The Biseks bravely fought the hostile regime and are now coming back victorious." Brave? Victorious? As if they had forgotten that our decision to leave the country was not motivated solely by the opportunity to stay in ministry, albeit abroad. We had succumbed to uncertainties and anxieties and therefore we could not possibly accept the label of heroes.

The variety of invitations was interesting. We were attracted to the Prague-Sporilov congregation because they invited us to a meeting with the session. When we met they told us about the congregation, their expectations and needs. I would wish that all candidates could see first of all what their prospective congregation sees as its needs and also difficulties and what its expectations and challenges are. About the rest, for example, where the manse is and so on, the candidate can find out if the appointment is likely to proceed. And so we began to plan to go to Sporilov.

The time until our delayed return was a time of special joy. We no longer found life in Scotland troubling. The pangs of exile had receded. We could try to live a full life as citizens of the United Kingdom. The institutional form of the Church both in Scotland and at home somehow resembled a family circle. And I was a little like the prodigal son who was coming home. Perhaps I had not squandered everything and I could even be useful. I remember an extremely positive remark someone made: "You're one of us. You haven't changed at all". In addition, we all felt we needed to return to the real Father. It was our common task. The tensions and altercations in the Evangelical Church of Czech Brethren only confirmed it. This was the time to prepare for the return home.

We were grateful that the Church of Scotland helped to pay for our removal to the Czech Republic. We were able to take all our books and also our upright Petrof piano, which managed to cross Europe twice and stay in excellent condition, although it meant hard labour for the removal men from Newcastle. They had to carry our piano without straps to the fifth floor up the steep and narrow staircase of the panel-block building in Prague. In some desperation they commented, "There are big lifts in every other building and we can also use our trolley and manoeuvre it easily there. We don't use straps at all." When they had delivered the piano to the flat with their bare hands, they collapsed with bottles of Pilsner in their empty van.

How was it with the saga of our removals? When the van got to Prague it was kept in the customs yard there, still with a seal on the door and a request that we pay a deposit of fifty thousand Czech crowns before anything could happen. We were told, "Don't worry, you'll get all of it back once we have checked that there is nothing out of the ordinary." The well-known "Don't worry" made us rather unsure. What could be out of the ordinary? How could we believe them? Why should we not worry? Why should we worry? It was a little too much for us with all the experiences we had had before we left the country in 1985. We refused to give them any money – we didn't have it anyway. And so we waited for three tense days, getting ready to file a complaint. When I finally went to enquire what was happening, a customs official snapped at me, "Just remove the seal!" I said, "But you're the only ones who can do it, aren't you?" He just said, "I'm not interested." So finally, we were able to start to settle into our flat in the 'Chodov II' housing scheme in the Southern City district of Prague.

There was a sequel to the saga of our removals: when organising our things, we found some crumpled lace underwear in one of the drawers – an obvious 'remnant' from the removal men's time of waiting at the Czech-German border crossing at Cinovec-Zinwald. They had to wait for us to get there with our documents, so that the van could be sealed, and only then were they allowed to enter the country. And, near the border, we saw with our own eyes scantily clad women swinging gracefully at the side of the winding road, ready for customers. We really felt ashamed. Was this what being home meant?

"So, are we back among our own people?" was the question we asked ourselves after the very warm welcome we received. Yes and no. Our experience had taught us that we could feel we were among our own only if we kept quiet when the talk turned political. We used to be asked, "What's happened? You left as opponents of Communism and now you've turned into socialists!" During our prolonged sojourn on the other side of the Iron Curtain the world of black-and-white had dissolved for us.

But homecoming was happy because there was a congregation that had invited me to become their minister. We first met during one of our annual visits to the Czech Republic and then they duly elected me as their minister. On our return, we were accepted into the congregation as if into a family. We had abandoned a very dear Scottish church 'family' at Govanhill Trinity in Glasgow, but we gained a new church family at Sporilov in Prague. We enjoyed gradually becoming part of a circle of friends. It was quite unexpected. When we were younger we weren't sure that close friendships with the minister could develop in his congregation. Life at home began to open up for us.

Our move into a high-rise block of flats ended our years of living in manses. The local congregation had first expected us to live in the manse, endearingly called the "wee manse". It contained two rooms, a kitchenette, a hall and a bathroom. Having in mind one of the predecessors who lived in the house some decades before, I felt I should not require more spacious accommodation. After all, there were just the two of us. But Daniela had a vision of the families of our four children coming for extended visits. To our satisfaction, thanks to a fund set up by a Dutch congregation to finance mission in the huge Communist-era housing scheme of the Southern City of Prague, the congregation was in a position to purchase a flat in Chodov II, which is a part of the Southern City.

The first ones to see the place were our two sons, Lukas and Benjamin. Their report was positive. They briefly described the three-bedroom flat on the fifth floor in Nechvilova Street and even took a few snapshots of the views from the windows to the south and to the north. Looking to the north you saw a larch tree very near the building which reached as high as the fourth floor. I remember how we spied on a woodpigeon's nest just a few metres below our window. But it was not without worries, because just a little further from the tree was the local boiler stack which was higher than our seven-storey building. It was a kestrel's favourite look-out. He had the woodpigeon's nest in full view. Our concern was justified; the nest was prematurely emptied and some chicks' feathers were scattered under the tree. Our son Lukas, who is an animal lover, said in a matter-of-fact manner, "And how do you think a kestrel should feed?"

Some tens of metres farther on was a car park. The view was very different from the one we had been used to in Teleci, which was my first congregation. There we looked at a green slope with woods at the top and from time to time we noticed some grazing deer. My last but one predecessor as minister had expressed how delightful the view from the manse was in a rather abrasive manner when a delegation from an industrial town came to invite him to become their minister. "Are you seriously asking me to exchange this view for your stinking town?" I heard this from the Teleci folk, who seemed to be boasting about it – but I felt rather embarrassed.

Let us return to the view from our flat in the Southern City scheme in Prague. There was a car park beyond the stack. I counted how many cars could park there and then I divided the number of cars in Prague by the number of spaces in the car park. The result was forty. Forty similar car parks. How long would it take before Prague became one large car park? After all, it is especially people living in a housing scheme who want to have a car. How else would they get to their cottages on Friday afternoon? Some time later, I became aware of a new paid car park with quite a lot of empty spaces. Then there was a series of broken windows in the cars parking on the street. Lo and behold, the paid car park filled very quickly. Was it only my overheated imagination that saw a connection?

Beyond the car park was a road leading to the Metro station. At that time, Daniela taught English at the Masaryk Institute of Further Studies in the city centre. Sometimes she had to leave very early and catch a bus from the nearest bus stop. Looking out of the window, I watched her running towards the road and, at the same time, as if watching a tennis match, I was on the lookout for the bus nearing the bend. I always tried to judge whether Daniela had a chance to catch it. Then I alerted her with a whistle (which I became an expert at while working in the woods round Teleci and it is our grandchildren who really appreciate my whistling and I like to show off) and then I saw how Daniela started running at full speed and got to the bus just as the door was closing. Sometimes, especially when it was cold, I hesitated whether to whistle or not. I thought, "There will be another bus in a few minutes, why should she be gasping for breath in a crowded bus and then be still wheezing in front of the students?"

About a hundred metres beyond the road was the D1 motorway. I used to tell our friends, "If you're planning to travel on the D1 on

Friday afternoon, give me a call. I'll look out of the window and tell you how long the tailback is, so that you won't be wasting your time and there'll be no danger of you losing your temper. Or would you prefer a bout of road rage?" How relieved we both were after coming to Prague to be able to get rid of our car, after having spent many years behind the wheel.

We could hear the din of the motorway which was amplified by the long rampart-like wall of the seven-storey buildings that lined it. You could not take it for the rustle of the trees or the murmur of the river or even the noise or roar of the sea. Only a summer thunder storm or fireworks on New Year's Eve on the other side of the building could rival the D1.

There was also a hillock on the north side of the building, slightly to the right, about forty metres high, getting overgrown with shrubs and bushes. A pagoda-like structure used to stand on its top. When the greenery had shed the leaves in the autumn, strange heaps of clothing, bedding and who knows what else were exposed. Was it left by a homeless person? Did the chill of the night force him to abandon the gathered or donated items? Getting rid of things seems to be as simple as dropping them without thinking, like an empty cigarette pack. I was irritated by the sight and had to clear the junk away. That was my obsession.

On another occasion, I remember doing Seniorat (regional Church Council) office work with my colleague Milos Rejchrt and, looking out of the window at some shrubbery in the field between the local road and the D1, we noticed some movement and when we looked closer we saw a tent-like construction and next to it a clothes-line with some items on it. We also saw someone on a bike riding through the grass. We concluded that it was a dwelling and that person's home. Some time later the field became a building site and we were very upset that he had lost his piece of land. This must be how people in Africa, Asia or South America lose their homes. I know that there are huge numbers of them, but we knew about the one near the motorway.

Today, the entire field is occupied by steel and glass office blocks. We can see white collars sitting in front of computer screens, mostly young men and women with a bright future; and I do not need to mention that I mean financial future for there is none other these days. Take a walk past the office buildings and see for yourselves how those who have made it are creatively exploiting the 'invisible hand of the market'.

And where is our man on the bike? Where is his tent or abode? And if he is on his way, where is his pillar of cloud by day and pillar of fire by night? What a dereliction of duty by both Milos and myself in the safety and comfort of our office to stop wondering about the fate of the homeless man.

There was also the view to the south from our windows on the other side of the flat. We could see green space encircled by other seven- or twelve-storey blocks of flats. The green space had an irregular shape and so the impression was not one of a military style set of buildings as many of our housing schemes tend to be. I once heard that before this housing scheme had been built (about 1984) the Communist Prime Minister Lubomir Strougal said, "We'll show the capitalists that we can build housing for our people." And I had a vision that on saying it he took out his wallet and shelled out the money needed. Was he not great?

The south side was the sunny side. The sun beat relentlessly on the walls of our block of flats. The higher it was, the warmer the flat. I remember how Daniela and I tried to escape the heat and find a shaded spot. The best seemed to be the nearby lake Sheberak with its cool water. But the discovery of fish with their bellies up and the inflow – a trickle of water running through a building site – confirmed that Lake Sheberak was not an ideal place. Perhaps it has changed by now for I would not like to spoil the nudists' enthusiasm. Their numbers were becoming overwhelming and you could encounter bare bodies not on only one, but on both sides of the lake.

I had an experience with the nudists at the Sheberak. It was a hot Sunday. I had preached for a colleague in Prague-Modrany and I was on my way home. Perspiring profusely I did not want to get home feeling so sticky and hot. I thought, "Why couldn't I join the nudists just for once? I'll carry the jacket in my hand and the tie will go in the bag with my robes. I'll have a wee swim, put on my trousers and shirt and dash home." And there I was, in my suit and tie among the naked bodies. I felt totally alien. My throat was tight with fear. Drenched in sweat I made haste through the strange naked swarm. Some were playing about with a ball, some just hanging around, and others were sunbathing. I saw things dangling and things protruding. My step was getting faster and soon I was running at undignified full-pelt. My relief was a cool shower at home half an hour later. And I had always thought that I could cope with nudity.

I would like to turn to the heart of our block of flats now. There was a tiny lift. The two wings of the door limited its space to such an extent that you could not even fit in a small washing machine, manhandling it up the steep staircase was the only solution.

Soon after we moved in, we noticed that every household was totally self-contained. What about the relationships between the different floors? Living on different levels made the separation even more explicit. It really was very different from the situation in a village. Do not be surprised that a villager does not know the word 'anonymity'. Now I understand why in Teleci the whole village was aware of the presence of the State Security who, trained in a town situation, kept their presence 'secret' by carefully changing their parking place along the same road.

A block of flats makes it possible to live a completely private life. It took us years to meet some of our neighbours. It is interesting how some people who live in the leafy parts of the city turn their backs on their neighbourhood by surrounding their detached house with a wall and installing an automatic gate. Our daughter-in-law, Adina, an architect specialising in city design and living and working in London, commented, "How come they get permission to build a wall like that? It's against the safety regulations."

To live in a block of flats is nevertheless to live in a community. By the smells you know what your neighbours are cooking for dinner. You share the commotion of visits, celebrations and parties and of arguments and rows. And there was something more specific, too. All flats had cable TV installed and everybody paid for the possibility to have all the channels that cable TV offered. We were very happy not to have a TV set at the time. So we wrote a letter saying that we felt we should not be required to pay the fee. The housing association representative, Mr Beranek, came to see us immediately and said, "You can't stop paying for your TV signal, because it would become more expensive for everybody in the building." Was it not clearly put? Did we think we lived just for ourselves? There were others to consider!

Soon we felt settled in the flat. It was comfortable. The clothes line was just outside one of the windows facing north. The doorbell chimed the moment Daniela started hanging some bed sheets out of the window. It was Mrs Vesela from the flat below us. She said,

"What are you thinking of? What about my view from the window?" I realised she meant the washing. So I asked her, "Could I see the angle, please"? "What angle? What do you mean?" she asked. Then she allowed me to look from one of her windows to see the flapping border of our washing some metres up. In the meanwhile Mrs Vesela kept on nagging, "And you've also flooded me." "Really?" I asked. "Can you tell me when it happened the last time?" "Two years ago," was her response. "But we moved in only two months ago," I said. "You see, you've managed it three times already," she said triumphantly. I left enlightened. We soon discovered that Mrs Vesela was rather unique.

There was another similar episode. On some evenings the floor of the flat served us as a space for playing bowling with plastic balls. The phone rang. Without an introduction Mrs Vesela said, "If you're doing what you're doing then stop doing it." It was more than a clear order; it is still used in our family. We felt embarrassed, laid a thick blanket on the tiled floor and carefully continued doing what we had been doing. On another occasion I sat at the piano in the middle of an afternoon and immediately heard banging on the pipes of the central heating. Without hesitation I ran down the stairs to ask Mrs Vesela what the problem was. "Do you think you can play whenever you fancy? What about your neighbours?" I replied with a question, "Are you watching a soap opera?" "It's none of your business," was her reply. I managed to say, "In that case I am free to play the piano any time between nine in the morning till seven at night". She gave me a sulky look and I took my leave. Since then, whenever I play the piano, and it is really only a few minutes once or twice a week, I think of Mrs Vesela, whether she is at home and what she might be doing.

We never happened to speak with most of our neighbours. Even if we took the short journey in the tiny lift together with another resident, we did not manage to get to know them. But we had an encounter with a woman from the next-door entrance. The family lived on the fifth floor as we did and one of their windows was next to our bedroom window. Their window was to the west from ours and the wind always blew in the direction from them to us. Having our bed right by the window meant that we would regularly be woken up by cigarette smoke. We had to share their breakfast of cigarettes. "What should we do about it? Should we ring their doorbell and speak to them? Would they become angry with us, because they wouldn't have time to consider what to say?" These were our deliberations and so we decided to write a letter explaining the situation and asking them if it might be possible for them to use another window. This was done and the letter was put in their letterbox. It was still on the same day when our doorbell rang and an angry woman said, "Why don't you just come and tell us you don't like our smoking? Why did you write us a threatening letter?"

The only occasion when the people from the three neighbouring entrances of the linked blocks of flats got together was a meeting which was called about once a year. It took place in the basement. It was a very unfriendly and depressing place, which was not conducive to any friendly conversation or discussion among neighbours. The matters to be discussed dealt purely with repairs and finance. The atmosphere used to be very cold and unwelcoming. There was also an aggressively outspoken man who, with depressing regularity, loudly voiced his frustration, commentaries and objections to anything. I remember how I once dared to ask him to be quiet, so that we could finish discussing a problem. His response was, "Oh, Mister Smarty Pants who knows how to do things. Look at him!" I realised how down there, in the basement, we were all pitifully equal.

I know that quite a number of those who grew up in a housing scheme have good memories of it. It is a proof of their ability to adapt and also of their good will too. Perhaps they are also able to reconcile with the environment in which they find themselves with kindness and even good humour, and expect and look for good things to happen. This is a promise for the future. But our friend, Revd Friedhelm Borggrefe from Ludwigshafen in Germany, once said that people would soon move out of the housing schemes. I myself do not think it will happen, because the style of living in a housing scheme meets some families' expectations. They have a place to go to after work and they are free to spend the weekends at their cottage in the countryside, or they can even stay at home (watching cable TV?).

As a minister trained in pastoral duties in Scotland, I tried to visit at least the members of our congregation in the housing scheme. But sometimes not even an invitation for a certain time meant that the visit would take place. As if the main door and doorbells were made of impenetrable concrete panels. How then can one share someone's joy or feelings of loneliness or sadness and unhappiness? I have had a vision that there must be a way to 'walk through' concrete panels. After an unsuccessful attempt to enter, I often left the locked door in self-pity which gradually transformed into grief at people living in the flats who did not know, and some of them did not want to know, what it meant to share one's burdens and how much pleasure it could bring to live in a community. There is a wise comment of our first President Tomas Garrigue Masaryk (1850 – 1937), who said that living in a city was like living in a desert – and yet, he never saw a high-rise block of flats.

Was there no joy? Oh yes, there was. Sometimes I was unexpectedly lucky in my attempts to visit. It also happened that somebody found us and came to our fifth floor. There were occasional meetings in our living room of some members of the congregation who called themselves the 'Middle Generation'. At the beginning of Advent the elders of the congregation met for a joyful evening of conversation and games. The group of young people in the church, mostly students, came regularly in the evening once a week for several years running. They enjoyed themselves and were sometimes quite noisy. I still do not understand why Mrs Vesela from the flat below us never banged the pipes or rang us when the young people were there.

Friends and guests from abroad also visited us in our flat. Once, the Moderator of the General Assembly of the Church of Scotland, Dr Alison Elliot, had a short afternoon rest in our bed. She was exhausted because she had to attend the funeral of Pope John Paul II during her short official visit in Prague. When she returned from her fleeting visit to Rome she told us that she had not seen another female participant among the many funeral guests. This rigidity of the church, and to be precise of our big sister the Roman Catholic Church, hurts me more than it irritates me. But we, both churches, also have lots in common as, for example we all try to reach people living behind concrete walls.

Chapter 20

MY MINISTRY IN THE CZECH REPUBLIC

So there we were. It was the first Sunday in the Sporilov congregation. In the middle of the service, an elderly woman fainted and fell down. There was a commotion; she needed urgent help. Fortunately, a doctor was present and, after the service was over, she told me that in a small space with low ceiling and many people present, such a situation would easily recur, especially in winter. It was the first signal that we would soon seriously discuss a more suitable space for the congregation.

There were also ordinary weekdays. We realised quite soon that contacts with members of our new congregation were a bit complicated, because the building where our flat was, was three kilometres from our small church. The motorway cut the parish in two and the bigger part was on the other side from our flat. I asked my friends in the congregation how to get to places. They said, "By car or by bus". "OK, but I want to ride my bike," I said. "But how will you cross the motorway?" asked the experienced natives, "There's no way of getting across!" To my satisfaction I soon found two pedestrian bridges and one flyover. Our bikes and the excellent public transport system in Prague made it possible for us to get rid of our car. We can still feel not only the financial but also the health benefits of that decision.

I began to introduce myself to the people on the roll and very soon knew that I could not apply my Scottish experience in Prague. The Scots opened their doors and I felt welcomed. Could the reticence that I often faced in my new charge be explained by the long-lasting pressure of the social circumstances? What I saw from the reactions in the housing scheme looked as if people had given up any belief in themselves, in their place in the world, in relationships; it seemed they had stopped seeing as mystery the existence of man and of the world.

Did it suggest that freedom meant that everyone should leave them alone? It looked like it. But the result was ending up in hopelessness and terrible loneliness. It hurt. The high-rise blocks intensified this feeling; as if not only the walls were made of concrete but the human hearts as well.

I still remember one of my first attempts to make a pastoral visit. I went to see one of the oldest members of the church. I came to a small house amid the high-rise blocks. There was a wire fence and a bell by the gate. Just as I was going to ring the bell, two fierce guard dogs appeared, growling and showing their teeth as if saying, "Don't you dare to touch the bell or we'll tear you to bits". I was frightened and put my arm down. When I tried again, their violent barking got even fiercer. I thought I would trick them by turning to them with my back. Then I tried to guess where the bell was and stealthily pressed it. I succeeded. The bell rang and the dogs went berserk. A window opened and an old man looked out. In a gruff voice he asked, "What d'you want?" I explained, "I am the new minister and I came to introduce myself to Mrs Novak. I found her name on the roll of the Evangelical Church of Czech Brethren." "She's dead." There was a short silence. I tried to continue, "I'm very sorry. Please accept my sincere condolences. Our records seem not to have been updated for some time." "And so what d'you want?" "I've just come . . ." "I've already told you she's dead." And the window closed again. I went away with my tail between my legs but lucky that I had not been bitten by the animals. My self-pity soon changed into thinking about the old man whose privacy was guarded by two fierce dogs and who wanted nothing to do with anybody else.

I also remember a faithful member of our congregation. He was in his late eighties. Once, when I went to pay him a visit in the block of flats where he lived with the family of one of his children, their neighbour told me that he had died several weeks before. When I went to express my condolences to his family, they welcomed me with the words, "You didn't know about it? It's a pity. He often spoke about you." I swallowed reproaching them for not telling me about their father's death. I could see that it had never occurred to them and it did not bother them in any way. It was only I who felt upset and sorry. As time went by, I often experienced that families did not feel the need for a formal ceremony, either a religious or civil one, to part with their deceased. I once mentioned it at our session meeting and said that it seemed that the dead were often thrown over the wall in the housing scheme. "Were you serious?" a member of the session asked some weeks later. How did I mean it, I the brute?

And there was yet another encounter which was exceptional but still rather typical. A woman came to the church office. No one had seen her in church as I later learned. Without introducing herself she asked whether I, the parish minister, always included chants in the Sunday service, where there was no room for them. I sensed a controversy and tried to tell her that chants were included when it was appropriate. I could not explain to her that most of them came from Africa and they made us realise that our way of worship was not the only one and certainly not the only right one. A warning question came, "And are you going to continue with it?" I said, "I don't know, I can't promise anything. Neither the session nor the members of the congregation have said anything against them." Her response was quick, "In that case I want you to strike me off the roll." I saw that there was no room for discussion. I took a piece of paper, sat at the typewriter and asked what her name was. The woman was indignant and continued, "What right do you have to do it? Do you think that people enjoy it?" Some time later an elder told me after a Sunday service, "Tomas, it's very interesting. I'm not good at singing but I really enjoy the little chants. I can sing them." This led me to thinking about the set order of our Sunday worship and how good it might be to step out of the ordinary and look for enrichment in preaching, prayers, singing and also sacraments, because an attempt to enliven the services could bring out a wider and deeper and perhaps even already half-forgotten meaning of our hymns, prayers and readings. It might also have the effect that people would stay awake or that they would not fall asleep so easily.

But there is more to it. It is stepping out of the church 'ghetto', which is difficult to do. It might be risky whereas it is cosy inside. We often understand one another even before we say anything. Another's reaction is usually sincere. We smile at one another. As if we always got on so well. As if we did not need to air the place, open the windows. What about pastoral visits then? What about mission in our resentful Czech environment? The fact that separation of the Church from the state has not been carried through has a negative effect as well because it aggravates the relationships between the Church and society. How do we respond to the indictment that the Church is only after money? Is it really not so? Has the Church and state separation not been discussed, as if it were only a question of reaching a financial settlement?

What about pastoral care and mission? That is a complex problem, because we have our jargon, our own language in the Church. We have our liturgical certainties. We have our status; we are kind and courteous, which is to our advantage. But all these attributes can stand as a barrier to a badly needed criticism, to confrontation and opening up. I remember a comment made by a Roman Catholic who once came to our Sunday service. She felt abashed when the door duty shook her hand to welcome her as if she was one of 'us'. She asked whether such cordiality would not discourage visitors. It is a hard question and I think that it is natural for us to welcome everybody. However, I would always call for restraint, appropriateness and respect for strangers.

I have a memory from my first charge. My father-in-law, an ardent member of the Church, would call out to a passing group of young people, "Are you coming to the youth club?" They looked at him blankly and went on. I felt very embarrassed. Similarly, a retired Scottish minister, who was one of a bus-load of Scottish visitors in the early nineties, walked through the village with his arms spread wide and with a broad smile. He embraced and welcomed everybody. I shrank within and did not know where to look.

The first place where we talked about the members of the congregation as friends was in the Sporilov church. Was it due to our age or experience or because the church was small, which strengthened the feeling of belonging? I remember what one of our youth club once told me, when I asked him whether there was someone else who also belonged to a Church in his school. "No, it's only me," was his reply. "Do you get mocked for it?" I asked him. "Sometimes," he said. "Do you mind it?" "I do, but they're stupid because they have no idea what it is about." Do we know what it is about? Do I know it?

My first Scottish colleague tried to teach me how to make the session decide in the way he would want them to. Once an elder of the church, Arthur Nelson, probably one of the oldest members of the session, told me, "But I'm not his Yes-Boy." He wanted to let me know how aware he was of being manipulated by the minister. I never wanted to have such a relationship with the session. But would I always be sensitive enough? Was I grateful enough to Pavel Hejda, the

Kurator (session clerk) in Prague-Sporilov, for being the chairman of the session and moderating all our deliberations?

I do not think that most of my colleagues in ministry would want to be above others, even in their professional knowledge and efficiency. I think most of them strive for equality with others and when there is something important to agree on, they try to explain the matter in a convincing way and look for understanding. Of course, arguments can always arise. Then it is necessary to distinguish strictly what is vital, what can be negotiated and what are only minor squabbles or whether somebody wants to force through his or her own idea.

Ministerial duties in the Evangelical Church of Czech Brethren seem to be endless, as they are also in the Church of Scotland, I believe. It is not at all easy to proclaim the Good News at Sunday worship. The living word is not so easily available. Moreover, it is to be proclaimed Sunday by Sunday. Really? Every Sunday? An older colleague of mine once remarked that a really good and meaningful sermon comes about once in ten. What about the nine others? What are the worshippers to do? How come some of them keep coming and wish their preacher well? Therefore I am convinced that it is proper to vary sermons, liturgies and prayers and look for enlivenment so that the participants await the Sunday service with anticipation. There is plenty of dramatic material in the Bible. It is true it takes some effort to access it. It also takes effort to imagine the listeners' side, try to understand their life situations and needs and, finally, listen to oneself and be reconciled to one's self.

There was one kind of service in Scotland, especially on the Island of Iona, about which the Evangelical Church of Czech Brethren harbours rather deep reservations. It was the service of healing. I felt rather doubtful at first, but the simplicity of the liturgy, laying on of hands and the prayer said over each one who came forward convinced me. The prayer went like this: "Spirit of the living God, present with us now, enter your body, mind and spirit and heal you of all that harms you. In Jesus' name. Amen."[1] It had nothing to do with charismatic and theatrical performance. I saw the gratefulness of those who had come forward and allowed others to lay hands upon them. We accepted this simple liturgy in the Prague-Sporilov congregation and once a month it became a part of the Sunday service.

---

1 From the Iona Community Worship Book, 1992.

It seems, however, that it is not easy for a member of the Evangelical Church of Czech Brethren to take part in something that is not 'intellectual'. Besides my experience in the Iona Abbey, I was helped by a member of the Govanhill Church, George, who owned a Newsagent's and worked there with his wife. He suffered from multiple sclerosis and the shop was getting too much for him. Once he told me, "Tomas, I know I will walk one day again." Neither of us said anything for a while. Then I said rather silently, "Yes, I know it too." And he told me that he attended a special healing service in another church once a month. He said it with apology, because we did not have such services in our church. I was very grateful for his openness. When I think back about the healing services we used to hold in Prague-Sporilov, I also remember some of those who used to lay their hands regularly upon those who needed healing.

Laying on of hands and physical contact in general, which, as we know from the Gospels, Jesus never shied away from, seem to have disappeared from our relationships. It is just one example of a broader problem. I would like us all to get nearer to the earthliness of the texts in the Old Testament. Now, when I had retired and experience the comfort of having time, I feel the need to follow closely the greatness of God's nearness to his people in the Old Testament.

Is it not the same with us as it was with the chosen people in the Old Testament? We also keep betraying God by our imperfections, our brutalities and our lack of faith. The Old Testament stories can be a mirror of our failures, our insecurities and sense of guilt. These inclinations are not somebody else's but our own. Through the Old Testament stories we can discover again what pride, hypocrisy or betrayal are like. We can read about love and passion, there are texts that are poetic, texts of wisdom; there are songs. We can bring the drama of the Old Testament stories to life, stories in which God was always with his people and came in flesh and blood in Jesus Christ, whom we want to follow. I think we need to face up to who we are in order that Christ's otherness and goodness is made manifest. It is his goodness and not ours. However, he can bestow it on us through his grace.

There were also other duties I was to take on. I felt more and more part of the community of my colleagues in ministry. Once they told me they would like to elect me as Moderator of the Seniorat (Presbytery) for the next six years, which entailed accepting responsibility for ministers and congregations in Prague and the environs. For me, to be in the position of Moderator meant pastoral care for my colleagues, some coordination of church life and taking services.

The decision-making body of a Seniorat is the Executive Committee, which is usually made of three ministers and three lay people who are elders in their congregations. I was very pleased to sit on the committee alongside my old friend Tomas Ruzicka. I remembered how he had come to see us in Teleci shortly before we left for Scotland. He had hoped to change our decision. He arrived and spent the whole day with us. He did not bombard us with countless reasons why we should stay. His friendly silence spoke volumes. In the afternoon, however, when we all went swimming in a nearby lake because it was a hot June day, his silent witness was broken. Enjoying the water and the sun, he suddenly called, "I can't get out. The elastic in my trunks has snapped." I do not remember any other words he might have uttered on that day. His saying so little, however, was a symbol of our understanding.

I know that I cannot expect that everybody would be generously tolerant and distinct in his or her silence in a mutual relationship and lasting friendship. As if there was a deeper challenge in it, a challenge, which society needs. Being blown off to a distant country, as happened to us when we lived in Scotland for eleven years, did not have to lead to a permanent separation. As long as we live, we cannot rule out new and renewed encounters. This is also what we read in the stories in the Bible. There are values that are brought out through meeting with those with whom we are willing to share our visions and values, our faith. The grace of God, who allows these encounters, is a sign for me that it is still possible to be a minister and preacher.

Chapter 21

THE CONGREGATION AND THE 'WALKING TOGETHER' CENTRE

Soon after I started working in the Sporilov congregation, discussions about the need to address the problem of church buildings resumed. There had been a plan of the congregation's Dutch friends who wanted to help to fund a new building which would serve both the church and the community. A dental surgery was to be part of it too. I saw a preliminary drawing of the plans for the 'House on the Hill' when by chance I paid a brief visit to a Dutch minister, Lowig Schoch, in summer of 1989. After the Velvet Revolution, however, the Dutch saw that their help was needed in orphanages in Romania. The Czech partners were to begin to act independently of Dutch financial assistance. Until the Velvet Revolution the Dutch had been absolutely constant in helping those who were in financial difficulties, usually for their political stance. They were most ingenious in making sure that those who were ostracised by the regime would not be left out. Dutch ministers who had spent one year of their theological studies in Prague at the Faculty of Theology were most able to find direct paths to those for whom they had some money while avoiding being checked by either the government or the fearful Church authorities. I admire the Dutch flexibility with which they evaluated the political change and began to direct their help elsewhere.

It was 1997. We learned about a Milena Svobodova, who had just succeeded in her search for a place where marginalised, ostracised and needy families would find refuge. There were plenty of them after the Czech and Slovak parts of Czechoslovakia split in 1993 and many people became stateless. Dual citizenship was not allowed and there were people who did not belong anywhere. The Prague Southern City Council offered the use of the disused and rather derelict premises of a former crèche which Milena would turn into accommodation for homeless families not all of which were of Roma or Czech origin. A never-ending whirl of events and worries began. Where would Milena get some funding so that the crèche could be transformed into a temporary home for homeless families? Where would she find money to run the place? Society had not devised a mechanism which would save Milena from endlessly writing up projects and filling in applications for grants, to allow her to devote all her energy to providing targeted care for those who were struggling and who encountered endless obstacles in their way, which she longed to remove.

Milena and the Sporilov congregation happened to set out on a journey together. The beginning was Milena's invitation for us to see the newly-acquired building. A member of the Session, Eva Grollova, and I went to look at the new place. Milena sketched out for us what basic refurbishment would be needed to make it fitting for the community of homeless families. We looked at the rooms and bathrooms, toilets for three-year-old children, kitchen equipment, furniture and other things. Eva Grollova, who was at that time the coordinator of Dutch foundation for the development of social projects in Central and Eastern Europe, was to evaluate the project and recommend a subsidy. Eva radically increased Milena's carefully weighed request for financial support, so that a thorough and appropriate reconstruction could take place.

In the weeks that followed we could see how Milena creatively engaged the new residents in reconstructing their temporary home. I saw again and again how she worked among those whom we were so good at avoiding and whom we ignored, of whom we were afraid. They wielded spades, brushes, trowels, locksmiths', electricians' or plumbers' tools and made the derelict space into something habitable. To experience Milena's relationship and communication with people who were down and out was unique. Her skill, which she had developed during her acting career, was reinforced by her passion for the marginalised. We were relentlessly pushed beyond our congregational comfort zone. The typical evangelical complacency, characteristic of life in a church ghetto, was broken down. It was time to prepare for our transfer to the Southern City. Milena and her protégés were already there, and yet they were still on a journey. We would soon understand that Milena was well aware of their need for Moses' pillars of cloud and fire if she and those she had taken under her wing were to continue their journey together. Were we, the 'respectable Christians', willing to look up to see these pillars and follow them?

Milena started to attend our Sunday services and then even became a member of the church. Thus she also shared with the congregation the dilemma of what to do with the old building constructed by the congregation in the 1950's. Should we build a new one or try to save the old one? Finally Milena posed an interesting question, "Why don't you build in our garden next to us?" I was dumbfounded. Then I said, "What good would it do? Do you really think that our middle-class and rather self-centred congregation could help people on the street?" "Certainly," she said. "They need to see that it is possible to live in a different way." I am still fascinated by her optimism. Or was it an expression of a wild hope?

I told the Session about Milena's suggestion and then also the congregation, in words I hardly recognised as coming from me. I said, "I can't decline such a Christian challenge. I don't know any other way of following Christ." There was no objection. How could there be? Our deliberations suddenly took a radical turn. The idea remarkably coincided with an offer from the Bavarian Evangelical Lutheran Church to give the Evangelical Church of Czech Brethren a significant financial gift on the tenth anniversary of the Velvet Revolution.

The Southern City of Prague, a large housing scheme for eighty-five thousand people, had been the focus of the ecumenical department of the Evangelical Church of Czech Brethren for several years. Therefore the Sporilov congregation, whose parish encompassed also the Southern City, was approached with the question of whether it would be able to accept the gift from Bavaria and plan the construction of an appropriate building. Some years before there had been an unsuccessful ecumenical project by both the Roman Catholic and our Church to have an ecumenical centre in the housing scheme. The project had not been realised due to lack of good will over the sharing of premises. Anxiety is often a hindrance to such ventures. Would we be fearful too? Accepting the gift from Bavaria meant a promise to set out on a journey.

Following Milena's invitation to become the neighbour of the homeless families, and with the Bavarian donation, architect Jiri Vesely started work on the proper plans. He had already worked on the reconstruction of the old church building in Sporilov. He was delighted that he was given the chance to work on a new church building and admitted that it had been his life-long dream. We were very fortunate that the city authorities were favourably inclined to having a new church in the housing scheme. Moreover, they even demanded that the architect should plan a reconstruction of the centre for homeless families, so that it would not look too small next to the church and that both buildings should create a harmonious whole.

The first thing to happen was a conference of the representatives of the local authorities and parties from abroad (Germany, Switzerland, Scotland) who were our potential sponsors. We met at the centre for homeless families; what better place would there be for this kind of meeting? Being aware that the Church's influence in Europe was on the decline, our foreign friends stipulated that they would not support the construction of a new church building if it was to serve the church family only. They did not seem to be convinced by our pointing to the fact that both the centre and the congregation had already set out on a journey together. They expressed their doubts that our project would be anything more than a mere vision. We all knew that it was natural to feel a great deal of hesitation about the beginning of a way not yet travelled. The Swiss representative of the HEKS organisation, Andreas Hess, was rather disparaging of the project. Friedhelm Borggrefe, Westphalia Church dean, was not less critical than Hess but, at the same time, he was also positive. This is what he wrote in his report about the consultation: "... In spite of all the problems, it is possible to recommend the project for realisation, because there is an excellent chance to look for a positive solution to the difficult situation of such a housing scheme. Moreover, it is also a challenge for the protestant churches of Europe to build a symbol of solidarity and hope at a very particular place which is one of the largest housing dormitories in what used to be the Eastern Block. If churches and congregations are willing to support one small community, so that their church will become a place of communication for a lot of people, then this project will become a project for the future...." Both Hess and Borggrefe together with those they represented became the most faithful and constant partners of the project and the most diligent organisers of fundraising.

I remember well how I anxiously weighed up the ability of our congregation to open itself towards those who had invited us through Milena to become their neighbours. How would we cope with the social differences? How would we approach those towards whom most of us felt inhibited, unsure and also, to a certain degree, incapable of giving support?

The time of preparing for the construction proved to be pleasing because it was a period when the two incongruous groups were getting to know one another. We began to visit the residents in the Centre, especially the children, most of whom were Roma. We played with them and sang and were getting used to their relentless restlessness. They always liked to sing chants, most of all those from Africa. We would sing them in the original language in our way, of course, and then in Czech. I still hear the little Roma children calling to me, "Mr Bisek, let's sing Sumisa." They loved the South African chant 'Amen, Siakudumisa'. It had been sung at the consecration of Desmond Tutu as Archbishop of Capetown. Tutu, a close friend of Nelson Mandela, and a man of indomitable courage and a child-like heart, could not restrain himself and began to move in time to the music and the congregation joined him and began to dance too. The culture of Africa entered the liturgy of the tame white Anglican Church. The captivating chant helped me to accept the Roma children's inextinguishable enthusiasm. Some young people and also adult members of the congregation took part in the work with the children. In conjunction with Milena and the residents of the centre we managed to organise gatherings of all sorts, sometimes also with visitors from abroad. A number of people were happy to be involved and Milena opened the centre to many possibilities. She was very tolerant towards our insufficiencies and tried to encourage us to carry on. She was always positive and overlooked our faults. It was not easy.

Milena knew very well how to deal with 'her flock'; she was one of them. She did not have to go far to find a fitting word or gesture which said it all. Her unwavering authority created a barrier against falsehood, violence, malice and laziness. She loved the people in her care and that was the key, together with her gift of insight into others. I remember a scene when we were at a meeting and the residents were finishing cleaning the yard before a celebration. Milena happened to look sideways through the open door and without warning started to roar, "Mr Telvak, what the hell are you doing?" It was a warm day and Mr Telvak, a pot-bellied Roma man who was the most ingenious of all in avoiding any physical activity, was lazily sweeping the yard and 'absolutely accidentally' drove all the dust against the open door and sparkling windows. On Milena's rebuke he indolently changed the direction. It was unbelievable even to see him at work. How come he was made to pick up a brush? The answer lay in what we all already knew: When Milena had the time she always worked alongside the residents as one of them. The consequence was that she often never got home at the end of the day. She stayed in the centre overnight, either because she had sensed there might be an emergency or because she was working very late on writing up projects and filling in applications for grants. Now and then exhaustion and her heart condition stopped her, which, in a way, was not surprising.

I also remember a late frosty winter evening. A social worker burst into the room where we sat talking. "Mrs Svobodova, there are three people standing outside. You know we can't take them in. It's not possible. Everything will be upside down again." Milena looked a bit embarrassed. After a while she said quietly, "But they will freeze outside." A couple with a child in their arms entered and Milena started to organize where to put them up. The family stayed for a number of weeks. She was able to deal with everybody in an impressive although sometimes very agitated way, but always in solidarity. She knew when to engage in negotiation. She sought new colleagues with great care, tried to give them her personal attention and counted on their commitment, integrity and dedication.

Very soon after the residential part of the centre was running, Milena set up a citizen's advice service which was free of charge for anybody needing the help of dedicated lawyers, some of whom gave their free time without remuneration. And so the association 'Walking Together' came into being.

The effort to gather enough money to begin the construction of our new church went on. We kept filling in applications to various church and secular bodies for grants or loans. Fortunately, we also made it onto the lists of the German foundation Gustav-Adolf-Werk and the Swiss foundation HEKS, which meant regular donations for the duration of the construction. We also received gifts from other German churches (Westphalia, Bavaria, Bremen and Baden). The

Board of World Mission of the Church of Scotland decided that part of the fund earmarked for mission in the former Czechoslovakia should be donated to us.

The House of Hope Church in St. Paul, Minnesota got in touch with us with a wish to visit and take part in the building process. A group, mostly students, arrived for a week of work experience. The young women did some imaginative decorating in the centre for homeless families and the young men helped on the building site. They found it amusing when one of the young Czech Roma helpers took a spade from the hands of his American counterpart and showed him 'the right way' to throw sand into the mixer. The group wanted to experience what life in a housing scheme was like. Therefore we had arranged lunches in the canteen of the local primary school. The first meal we had was mushy peas and frankfurter, which our American guests found very difficult to cope with. Among the American party there was a retired school headmaster. I saw him standing in the corner of the school dining hall watching the children queuing to get their lunch and then sitting down and eating. I was curious and when I approached him he said, "You have wonderful children." "No doubt you have wonderful children too," I replied. "No, they're rascals. No, in fact, not they but their parents. Nothing is ever right for them and they negatively affect the running of the school." The House of Hope Church kindly remembered us and sent us several donations towards the building fund.

We also received a very different visit. It was a group from a Presbyterian Church in Ponca City, Oklahoma. It was as if a school party was on an excursion. They arrived, looked at the site, consumed lunch prepared by the resident women of the Centre and left.

A lasting solidarity that we were aware of came from the Iona Community. We received a gift from their central fund and some of the Family Groups of the Community kept sending us cheques together with personal letters at the time of disbursement of funds.

The Swiss Reformed Church in the Canton of Nidwalden aimed to establish a lasting relationship with a congregation of a Reformed Church in what used to be Eastern Europe, and with the help from Andreas Hess they twinned with our congregation. Andreas used to visit us quite regularly and in an excellent way balanced his critical view of our project with negotiating how to help us. When I wondered about it, he told me that his daughter was in Romania working with orphaned children and so he obviously had a soft spot for Roma children suffering hardship. Once Andreas happened to see 'our' homeless children dance and sing and he watched them with great interest. The folk from Nidwalden came to see us on several occasions. They kept encouraging us and also helped us with financial gifts. One of their ministers, Jacques Dal Molin from Buochs in Nidwalden, had his own experience with Roma people from Slovakia. Buochs is a village near the motorway to Italy. After the political changes in 1989, the Slovak Roma could travel freely and they looked for work elsewhere in Europe, including Italy. On their way they used to stop at the manse in Buochs to beg for money. They could not speak German but knew a few words like 'hungry', 'family', 'work', 'please'. Jacques always tried to find a small job for them to do and so earn a little money. Some were good at working in the garden. Others did not want to do anything. After some time the Swiss police arrived at the door of the manse with the question, "Is it true that you give work to foreigners? It's a criminal offence." Jacques then did not know how to explain to the Slovak pilgrims that he was no longer allowed to let them earn some money.

Our architect, Jiri Vesely, accepted an invitation to visit the Evangelical Church in Westphalia to look at their new church buildings. This showed their approval of Jiri's plan for our new church. Jiri was very pleased and wanted to accept the invitation but admitted that he did not speak any German. So I joined him, and we travelled together to Westphalia. I was fascinated by how Jiri's lack of competence in German changed into a lively communication with his German counterparts when they discussed architecture in the churches we visited.

The period of endless filling-in of applications, accepting gifts of money, sending thank-you letters to the kind donors and also countless visits of persons or representatives of institutions was exhausting. But our project and the 'Walking Together Centre' were given constant support. Groups from the German organisation Gustav-Adolf-Werk and Diakonia directly expressed their satisfaction at our project.

The gift of a pair of church bells was totally unexpected. They were donated by a retired German minister Heinz Raulf and cast by Czech Master Bell-caster Rudolf Manousek in the Netherlands. Our youth group gave them the names Mary and Martha. At the time

CHURCH AND THE 'WALKING TOGETHER' CENTRE

when our cooperation with the 'Walking Together Centre' was at its best, I tried to understand which one was the hard-working and caring Martha, and which one was the listening and cared-for Mary.

The fact that the funds for the construction were insufficient was obvious and so the congregation decided to sell the old church in Sporilov. With the very efficient help of some members of our congregation the process kept advancing and finally, we were ready to choose a building firm, the spade hit the turf and the construction started. It was the autumn of 2002.

Suffering from multiple sclerosis, architect Jiri Vesely started to live in the 'Walking Together Centre' so as to be close at hand and be able to oversee the work done on both the church and the centre. Just as Milena had, so he too gave all his time to the projects, amending the plans and making sure the work was done as it should be.

Having sold the old church building in 2003, the congregation became homeless, and as a homeless family, we accepted accommodation at the 'Walking Together Centre', where we met for our Sunday services and other occasions until the completion of our building in 2006. I like to remember this time because the congregation was forced to look beyond themselves. Being in frequent contact with life in the centre, we saw the social workers' openness. All of a sudden we had a chance to get closer to the problems of those who may never have heard a kind word, or to do for others what Milena enabled them to do for us and our guests. They were proud to open their tidy rooms to our guests from abroad; they baked cakes, the children sometimes showed us how naturally gifted they were at dancing. The occasions spent together were both informal and festive. The Sunday services in the meeting room of the 'Walking Together Centre', when we had to fit into a small space which always had to be set up from scratch every time for worship, were special in as much as we were only guests in the place and close to one another.

It was mainly due to the people in the 'Walking Together Centre' that our kind donors kept being open towards our needs. They also began to understand a certain rhythm in our demand for support. Our faithful benefactors from Westphalia commented on it in this

TOMAS BLESSING THE CROSS
ON THE NEW CHURCH SPIRE

way, "When we want to undertake such a project, first we prepare everything carefully, then work out the cost, find the money, and only then carry it out. Whereas you carry out only what you have money for and then look for more." But it was not only money or the lack of it which the progress of the construction depended on. It was also the speed with which our architect kept finalising each step of the plan. Then he discussed the material to be used, the methods to be followed and, of course, the cost. I remember our regular meetings where we discussed each item separately. Jiri, the architect, tried to defend his ideas of appropriate quality and the visual aspect and I found it extremely difficult to rein him in. Jiri's health deteriorated to such a degree that he was not able to finish the church in all its details so as to hand over his completed work. Just as the cross on the spire of the church was to be erected, Jiri died. It was on the 9th January 2006.

It was a colleague of Jiri's, architect Professor Petr Keil, together with Jiri's son Vavrinec, a student of architecture, who was able to take over the job and finish it. We were grateful to them all for the building in which we enjoyed meeting for worship and other events.

The church headquarters were not very happy that so much foreign funding had gone in our direction although they were involved at the very conception of the plan to build a church. However, they did not subsequently show any interest in the process until it was finished. Of course, the final cost kept rising, as so often happens with such a big project as ours. Jiri, the architect, was indomitable in his zeal to make use of the most advanced technical equipment, which was a source of many arguments between the two of us. Some of my objections still hold; for example, I was very much against the installation of air-conditioning and windows that cannot be opened in a space where people meet a couple of times a week for a few hours at a time, in an environment where there is greenery around. On the other hand, the building as such has received many favourable comments and is much appreciated.

Our journey from the old church to the new drew to an end. Completion of the new church meant that we were no longer homeless. The congregation had a new house and was very happy to move those ten metres that separated the 'Walking Together Centre' from the church. Unfortunately, we also stopped being so close to the residents as there seemed to be much to do with getting settled and organising our church life. Is it not being on a journey that stimulates, nourishes and encourages a community? Whereas being settled and comfortable weakens our initiative, our willingness to look out for a direction and stay on the way. I was very worried whether we would be able to keep up a creative relationship of the two communities, between the homeless and those who were secure and comfortable.

Not long after I retired, the new leadership of the local authority closed down the 'Walking Together Centre'. It was the end of a remarkable service to the needy, when they were helped to begin to live independently and fully. Helping homeless families did not end with the changed situation. But what can be done for those who need care is very much curtailed, as they now live in eight flats scattered from one end of the city to the other. As I look at the way in which the communal life of the 'Walking Together Centre' and the congregation came to an end from the distance of the horizon beyond our time, I feel the need to express my thankfulness to our Lord for the twelve years of favour. I see God's grace physically present in the bas-relief at the entrance to our church sanctuary, which represents the torn curtain in the Jerusalem Temple at Jesus' crucifixion. It is the torn body of Christ through which we enter and which reminds us that the world and the church are one. The torn curtain is a promise and also our hope which we cherish.

Chapter 22

CONCLUSION, 2014

Approaching the end of my journey, I see that I am still searching and still trying to find the way. There is one prevailing feeling which keeps returning, perhaps a little clearer now than it was when my search began. I recognise that at the decisive turning points of my life, when I had to make a choice and I found a new direction, my hesitations and uncertainties ceased. Amazingly, what had seemed to be a tentative and perhaps even reckless move subsequently turned out to be the appropriate progression, a path illuminated for us. Daniela and I both believe that our direction was given to us. I know that this feeling cannot be proved, empirically verified or validated beyond question. And yet, it is what I want to share.

In this context I see three main episodes of my life. The first one comes from Teleci, the little village in the Bohemian Uplands where I served as a Presbyterian minister. I vividly recall the wonderful reaction of the elders of the Teleci congregation to the pressure from the hostile authorities. Most of the elders were farmers, with the ground cut from under their feet during the collectivisation of farming in the 1950s. They unexpectedly responded in an absolutely free and courageous way, contesting fabricated accusations against their minister. The light shone through the darkness and the path we walked along together was illuminated. We were certain that our direction was approved and hope was given to us, albeit for only that short and fleeting moment. However, we experienced a foretaste of the fullness of eternity to come.

The next episode was very different. It lasted the whole length of the eleven years during which we, as a family, lived in Scotland. Having been expelled from Czechoslovakia, we felt uprooted in many ways, we grieved over our sorrowful lot, and yet we found ourselves being fully accepted by the Scottish people. Working as a minister in the Church of Scotland, and therefore meeting a variety of people and coping with a range of problems on a daily basis, I never felt that I was not accepted. Yes, the light was shining on my path. I was never regarded as someone alien or strange or unwanted. I was one of those who walked together as one community looking forward to an even greater gathering at the final feast.

The twelve years following our return to Prague have been the final episode. Then I witnessed the coexistence of two very different communities – the community of the church and the community of homeless families, when the congregation came to settle next to a centre for homeless, downtrodden and destitute people in the Southern City in Prague. Building our church in their intimate proximity, in order to share their lives, was something absolutely new to everyone. Sharing in various events meant breaking down barriers. Of course, I also remember many serious challenges we faced, but the light was shining throughout those years nevertheless.

The light will not shine in the church if it remains separate, curtained off, from the secular world. The torn curtain is beautifully embodied in sculpture at the entrance to the sanctuary of the new church in the Southern City. It symbolises the torn body of Christ, the guarantor of unity – in this case, unity between the well-established and the destitute. May our paths lead us by means of the torn body and may we find the light shining on both 'sides'. Yes, the world and the sanctuary belong together as we all do.

Eight years have passed since we walked through the torn curtain of that church for the first time in 2006. That unique doorway into unity is not readily at hand for us now. We had to move to yet another place and try to settle there and feel at home. Have we managed to settle? Can we say it is our home? Or shall we repeat with confidence that there is no place of lasting abode here on earth as we wait for the last and permanent home?

Let me name again the places in which Daniela and I have lived together. The first one was the Huss' Halls of Residence, boisterous, merry and somewhat chaotic, where we shared our life as a newly married couple with other students of theology. It was much easier for me than for Daniela because I was 'one of them'. She, however, due to her kindly determination to look on the bright side, recalls with pleasure the sometimes mischievous interactions there.

Our next dwelling place was a part of a little flat in Kremencova Street opposite the 'U Fleku' brewery and pub. The pub was always packed with customers, a good number of them foreigners. It was always very late when the pub closed and the intoxicated clientele walked home in a very merry mood. How could you sleep then? The Czechs looked for pebbles to throw in the direction of our second-floor window after I had tried to pour cold water on them. On the other hand, when the Germans identified the problem, they organized themselves into a squad-like formation and marched away. An interesting difference!

Then it was Union Theological Seminary in New York, where our home was in a spacious flat for the next year. There were three of us – Daniela, our baby daughter Lucie and I. Having more space than we needed gave us the opportunity to accommodate two new Czech immigrants, a mother and her little son who were trying to settle in New York. Also our Scottish friend, Andrew Hunter, a chemical engineer, lived with us for a short time. He amazingly got permission to visit us in our first long-term home in Teleci after our return to Czechoslovakia in 1970. He was on his way from the Philippines, where he had worked as an oil expert. He thought it was harsher to live under the spiritual oppression in Czechoslovakia than under the martial law he had just experienced in the Philippines.

And yet, in Teleci we were so happy and grateful for all the beauty of the place, and perhaps even happier when we had our four children. They were a marvellous stabilizing factor during the time of the constant surveillance by the State Security. We felt that God was right there with us especially at the critical moments of our encounters. And so he was, we keep reminding ourselves, and he still is in his hidden and yet very distinct way. Can we really be sure of that, having felt like unwanted squatters and having been forced to abandon our country? Of course we can, even more so now, when we look back and see how he has straightened our paths and made them meaningful for us.

Our first Scottish home was in Balloch-Eastfield in Cumbernauld, where we felt so bereft of our mother tongue and longed for our families and friends left behind the Berlin wall, which divided Europe into two crippled parts. Now, after many years, I see it is important to accept one's smallness and even inferiority in a new place. This was what Pedro Arrupe knew so well when he sent his Jesuit brothers to countries about which they knew next to nothing. It is in these circumstances that one learns to appreciate the extremely precious gift of the human Word that has been given to us. As we read in St John's Gospel, "In the beginning was the Word . . . and the Word became flesh . . ."

From Cumbernauld we moved to Glasgow. That was significant for us because we lived as citizens of the country which adopted us and we felt an obligation to carry the burdens of daily life alongside others. From that we learned that if those who have lost their homes can be willing to share in the everyday burdens of others, they are enabled to live their lives in the fullness of the new situation. Life is not to be hoarded as something only we deserve, and nor is it to be taken for granted.

To say farewell to our new found home in Scotland was not easy. Nevertheless, Daniela and I felt we had unfinished business in the Czech Republic, where we had spent the bigger part of our lives. Of course our four adult children had to decide where they belonged, a problem which we, as their parents, could not resolve on their behalf. They have their whole lives in which to find an answer to the question. Yes, I mean their lives from the very beginning to the very end, not just a part of them but the whole thing, because life is a gift given to each of us.

So here we are, now back in Prague again, living in a little house with a patch of garden, in a quiet *cul de sac* with friendly neighbours. We are grateful for the feeling of being fully settled in our latest home. It is not our only home, because our four children have established themselves in four different places around the British Isles: our daughters live in Scotland and our sons in England. There are twelve grandchildren in the four families and we feel at home in all four of them.

When we travel back to Prague, we sense that we are also on our way home again. That sense is not of our making, though. Is it a coincidence then? And if it is not a coincidence, then we are, hopefully together with you, on our way to the heavenly home: the final one, the place which is prepared for us all.

Appendix 1

REPORT BY STATE SECURITY ON TOMAS BISEK, 1971-86

The document which follows has been copied and translated. The underlined parts were underlined by the original writer. The parts in brackets and in italics are the translator's explanations of abbreviations and of some terms. At the end of the document there are lists of names. The list of contacts' names in Czechoslovakia was omitted as superfluous.

Regional Headquarters of State Security in Hradec Kralove, Division II, Department 2

15th August 1986   Strictly Confidential

EVALUATION of Personal File "SAMOTA" (*"The Remote Place"*), No. 9736

Hereby I present for approval the evaluation of personal file No.9736, which deals with:

BISEK Tomas, born on 30/11/1939 in Prague, of Czech nationality, no registered citizenship, married, former minister of the Evangelical Church of Czech Brethren in Teleci, former address Teleci 129, Svitavy, a signatory of Charter 77, a member of the *New Orientation*, emigrant, permanent address 82 Cairngorm Gardens, Balloch Eastfield, Cumbernauld, Great Britain, registered as HP (*Hostile Person*) of 1st category.

Work on the named person began on 15th April 1971 in Surveillance File at the Svitavy Police Headquarters, because he spent one year of post graduate studies in the USA at the Union

Theological Seminary, in the Ecumenical Fellows Programme in New York after graduating at the KEBF (*Comenius Evangelical Theological Faculty*) and <u>because his brother Petr emigrated to the USA</u> in 1965, where he still lives. <u>Father Frantisek BISEK was under surveillance in 1958-1959 in action MECHANIC</u> on the basis of information that he was <u>marked for cooperation</u> with Intelligence Service when on a business trip to Switzerland in 1954. The case was closed after an interrogation of F. BISEK, who denied everything. As a result, F. BISEK was dismissed from the Ministry of Construction and expelled from the CPC (*Communist Party of Czechoslovakia*).

Work on T. Bisek was first focused on documenting his contacts with citizens of Czechoslovakia and also VF's (*Visa Foreigners*). Then there was the evaluation of the activities of a former resistance group

186

directed from Great Britain, Intelligence Service under the name R3. Some of its members who come from around Teleci are still alive but are very old and it is not anticipated that they could be active against the state.

On the basis of existing knowledge about the Subject, his file was transferred to "signalled" on 7/11/1973, and to "personal" in April 1974. Then it was found out that BISEK had gathered a group of young ministers of the ECCB – Miloslav PLECHACEK, Jan KELLER, Bohdan PIVONKA and Pavel HLAVAC. All of them formed a compact and completely compatible group. Intelligence documented that all of them frequently visited one another and these visits very often turned into meetings. According to the obtained intelligence, it was documented that the Subject and all the other named persons displayed hostility which can be characterised as subversive.

The Subject belonged to so-called "The New Orientation", a group of radical orientation. It was found out that there were contacts made with the representative Jakub Trojan HP (*Hostile person*). At the same time, meetings of supporters of HP's (*Hostile persons*) took place at the Subject's and the KELLER's. Source DIAGRAM reported the Subject and his confidential contacts' harsh attacks on the USSR and the socialist regime in the CSSR (*Czechoslovak Socialist Republic*). It was found out that the whole group round BISEK sent a letter of protest against the way the ECCB's (*the Evangelical Church of Czech Brethren*) Synodal Council had dealt with the matter regarding TROJAN in 1974. It was also noted that the Subject also had active contacts with members of HP's (*Hostile persons*), MILOS REJCHRT and VOJEN SYROVATKA.

The Subject was very active in youth work. He was a member of the Youth Committee at the ECCB's Synodal Council. With the help of his wife he organised so-called Sunday Schools, bible studies, trips to important sights and to other ECCB congregations, etc. The Subject was a regular listener to foreign seditious broadcasts – Radio Free Europe, The Voice of America, London and Deutsche Welle. It was also noted that the Subject and groups of younger ministers of the Policka District stood up for teaching religion to children in the Manses.

The Subject attended a meeting of HPs (*Hostile persons*) in Opatov in September 1974, where the socialist regime of the CSSR and the current situation in the ECCB were criticised. It was noted that in October 1974 the subject had contact with the "spiritual father", emigrant LOCHMAN HP (*Hostile person*), whom he met when he studied in the USA. Another meeting of HPs (*Hostile persons*) in Libstat in February 1975 was dispersed by police intervention. After the event BISEK wrote a letter of protest to the Regional Clerk for the Supervision of Churches in Hradec Kralove after a consultation with another member of HPs (*Hostile persons*), SLAMA, who advised him to publicise the whole thing and put an appeal in the papers and also send it to the Central Authorities. Because of these facts BISEK's position allowance was lowered by KCS200, about which he complained to the District Authorities in Svitavy.

On 16/9/1975 Bisek was visited by HULBERT VF (*Visa Foreigner*) in the Manse. HULBERT asked the Subject to pass on news about the Churches's and political situations and offered him larger amounts of money from Free Europe. BISEK tried to cover up the visit. At this time, the group round BISEK proposed a motion at the district Church meeting to be discussed at the next meeting of the Synod which described the current situation as discriminatory and against the conclusions from the conference in Helsinki. In April 1976 BISEK told the elders at their session meeting about the anniversary of the death of Palacky (translator's note: *Frantisek Palacky, 1798 –1876, was a Czech historian and politician, the most influential person of the Czech National Revival, called "Father of the Nation"*) and likened the conditions of that time to the conditions of today because of censorship. At this meeting he also organised a letter of protest to the District Authorities in Svitavy against his position allowance having been taken off his pay. Moreover, he also gave the participants political information which he got from listening to foreign broadcast, especially Radio Free Europe. In October 1976 BISEK received 13.000 Tuzex Crowns from an unknown donor abroad.

The Subject attended Svatopluk KARASEK's trial and together with KELLER and HLAVAC made copies of a hostile report on the proceedings and also the content of declarations of protest. The Subject and his wife did not attend the elections of people's representatives and thus influenced several students at the Comenius Evangelical Theological Faculty who, as a result, did not attend the elections either.

In 1977 BISEK, KELLER, PIVONKA and also HLAVAC signed the pamphlet CHARTER 77. BISEK explained his signature as an act of solidarity with other signatories of CHARTER 77. He had thought that there would be unleashed a severe action against the signatories and they would be liquidated and therefore he wanted to support them. In June 1977 BISEK composed an explication of some questions which TROJAN later used in Document No 9 of CHARTER 77. At the same time, TROJAN decided that a group of CHARTER 77 signatories from the ECCB would petition the Federal Assembly because of cases where the Church was persecuted or discriminated against. This petition was signed by BISEK, who also took part in its preparation. Other signatories were also HLAVAC and PIVONKA. A copy was sent to the WCRC in Geneva. It was found out that the Subject had contact with SABATOVA-UHLOVA at his address in June 1977. BISEK and his wife's passports were confiscated in August of the same year. His wife also signed CHARTER 77, her signature appeared in Document No. 11. BISEK distributed CHARTER 77 documents Document No 12, Information about CHARTER 77, Revocation of BREZINA's draft notice and Professor Komarkova's paper „Difficile Est". BISEK and the other signatories of CHARTER 77 from the ECCB were punished with a reprimand by the Synodal Council. It was found out that BISEK had contact with the right-wing journalist Otka BEDNAROVA at the turn of 1977 and 1978. It was partially documented in the presence of the Subject on 12/4 and 13/4/ 1978 that the pamphlet CHARTER 77 was distributed among believers in the form of notes from an interrogation testimony. Partial PCM (Preventive Corrective Messure) was carried out under Criminal Code 40/74 Coll. Section 19. Then BISEK wrote a letter to CHARTER 77 in which he described the methods used by the security as a serious interference in the Church's activities. In May BISEK distributed materials of CHARTER 77 among DDR nationals. BISEK, his wife, professor VYDRAR and Pavel HLAVAC signed a letter of protest to theRegional Prosecutor in which they asked for the release of Jan SIMSA, a minister of the ECCB. An interrogation of BISEK was carried out under Criminal Code 40/74 Coll. Section 19 on 27/7/1978. He admitted that he had contacts with VF (*Visa Foreigners*). He admitted signing CHARTER 77 but refused to specify the place and the time of signing. He also admitted informing the leadership of Charter 77 about the interrogations of the elders of the congregation. He also visited HAVEL the writer in April 1978, allegedly in order to hear the concert of the group the PLASTIC PEOPLE. He refused to comment on his contacts with Petr UHL. In September 1978, BISEK attended a meeting of signatories of CHARTER 77 from the ranks of the ECCB at the cottage of KELLER in Dolni Alberice, District Trutnov.

In February 1979, BISEK attended a meeting of signatories of CHARTER 77 in Brno at Jan SIMSA's, where the question of new spokespersons of CHARTER 77 was discussed, TOMINOVA, BENDA and DIENSTBIER. The Subject was visited by <u>KOSLOWSKY VF </u>(*Visa Foreigner*) <u>from GFR</u> during this month and BISEK informed him about the political situation in CSSR and the movement of CHARTER 77. On 15/2/1979 BISEK attended the trial with the spokesperson of CHARTER 77 Jaroslav <u>SABATA</u> in Hradec Kralove. Then he was present at the meeting of spokespersons and signatories of CHARTER 77 in the roadside cafe MAJAK near Hradec Kralove. On 17/2/1979, the Subject organised a meeting of young people from the congregations in the District which was also attended by <u>Jiri MÜLLER from BRNO</u>. They evaluated the situation in CHARTER 77 and among the signatories. Petr UHL and his wife visited the Subject in May 1979. All of them then visited another signatory of CHARTER 77 <u>HOMOLA</u> and they assessed the situation in CHARTER 77 and especially the CFDUPP (*Committe for the Defence of Unjustly Persecuted Persons*). They agreed that UHL, BISKOVA and HLAVAC would copy CFDUPP materials also for Brno, Pardubice, etc. Then UHL explained tensions in CFDUPP and how it is connected with Amnesty International. Frequent contacts with Anna SABATOVA from Brno were found out in May 1979.

On 2/7/1979, in agreement with the instruction from X of the NSF (*National Security Force*) in Prague, the Subject was interrogated to clarify his connections to the members of CFDUPP. The Subject refused to answer on the ground that he could cause his own criminal prosecution. In agreement with the instruction from X of the NSF (*National Security Force*) in Prague, and Directive No. 20/78 BISEK <u>was administered a caution</u> in the presence of the District Prosecutor on <u>6/7/1979</u>. He used CHARTER 77 to contend against the caution but acknowledged it.

A leading person of Culture II (translator's note:*Underground culture*) Karel <u>SOUKUP </u>(CHARLIE) stayed with the Subject from 15. to 17. 7. 1979. They discussed the situation in the CFDUPP (*Committe for the Defence of Unjustly Persecuted Persons*). It was found out that the Subject and his wife tried to organise a collection for the CFDUPP members in difficulties. In July the Subject was visited by <u>KESSLER VFs</u> (*Visa Foreigners*) from Switzerland. They talked about the situation of the Church in the CSSR, difficulties with theological studies, etc. The Subject also informed the visitors about CHARTER 77 and the CFDUPP.

He and other members of HPs (*Hostile Persons*) attended a ministers' conference in Vrbnopod Pradedem, where he presented his negative views and tried to distribute some CFDUPP materials.

There were several forced meetings with the Subject in the course of 1980 which, however, did not meet the expectations. The Subject remained hostile; he refused to respect the state authorities' regulations regarding reporting visits by VF's (*Visa Foreigners*). He continued to organise protest actions to change the state authorities, the Synodal Council, etc. He also organised protest actions against REJCHRT's, KELLER's, etc's state licences having been withdrawn.

In April 1980 there was a meeting of HPs (*Hostile Persons*) at the Subject's. More than 40 persons were present, including <u>KOCAB, TROJAN, HEJDANEK, SIMSA and CAPEK</u>. The participants tried to create an up to date plan which was against the new Synodal Council.

From18/8 to 24/8/1980, there was another meeting of HPs in Sumava, where the Subject and TROJAN had an argument. <u>BISEK</u> then <u>created his own group KELLER, BRODSKY, HLAVAC and PIVONKA</u>. The group supported unequivocally the Czechoslovak opposition and the movement of CHARTER 77. It was found out that the <u>Subject had contact with the former agent of the Czechoslovak espionage group in the non-Catholic churches, Jaroslav Cihak</u>, in the course of 1980, who was filed in the archives for unreliability.

During 1980 the Subject continued contacting Milos REJCHRT, who directly coordinated BISEK's activities. He also continued contacting Anna SABATOVAUHLOVA, for whom he found a summer cottage in the village of Baziny.

The Synodal Council began interviews with members of HPs (*Hostile Persons*), also with BISEK, in 1981.The Subject destroyed all materials connected with the dissident movement in the CSSR following the onset of the DELTA action. He showed concern about criminal sanctions against himself. He did not attend the elections of people's representatives yet again.

During 1982 he was actively in contact with members of the Czechoslovak opposition Anna SABATOVA UHLOVA, Pavel ROUBAL, Jiri MÜLLER, KELLER, Andrej LUKACEK, etc. <u>The Subject's state licence for ministry was withdrawn in May 1982 and he started to work as a forest worker</u> with the Forestry Company in

Policka. After his state licence for ministry had been withdrawn, <u>he received a considerable sum of Tuzex tokens</u>. It happened again before Christmas. The Subject bought a LADA car 2L03 with the number plate SYB4085. He had the money from <u>Svatopluk KARASEK in Switzerland</u>. He applied for the state licence for the vacant charge in Opatov in Jihlava District, which was, in cooperation with the state authorities, not granted to him. After <u>his state licence had been withdrawn, the Subject limited his open hostile activities</u> but did not change his opinion. He passed on his leading position as the organiser of HPs (*Hostile Persons*) and as a link between Prague and Brno to Bohdan PIVONKA. Although he did not act openly at this time, he still kept helping and supporting Anna SABATOVA and took part in the meetings of opposition in Svratouch which were legalised as bible studies, etc. The reason the Subject subdued his open activities in opposition was his endeavour to get back the state licence for work in ministry.

The Subject maintained frequent contacts with the opposition agents UHL, SABATOVA-UHLOVA, MÜLLER, PIVONKA, HLAVAC, SABATA, etc. during 1984. In September 1984 it became known that it was the Subject's intention to emigrate. Therefore he tried to get an offer of a minister's post with the help of his contacts in the Capitalist countries. He received an offer from the Scottish Reformed Church in October 1984 which he accepted. The Subject and his wife applied for the forms necessary for emigration in November 1984. The Subject, his wife and their oldest daughter, who was already 15 at that time, applied for permission to emigrate. After some forced contacts with the Subject, he and his wife <u>applied for the renunciation of their citizenships in March 1985</u>, which was granted to them. On <u>10/7/1985 the Subject and his whole family went through the Checkpoint Authority at Ruzyne and travelled to London and then to Cumbernauld</u>. The Subject and his wife left the CSSR <u>as non-citizens</u>. After his arrival in Scotland, several journalists visited the Subject, who used the opportunity for <u>slanderous articles in the British and Scottish press</u> which were <u>broadcast by the Radio Free Europe</u> on 19 – 26 August 1985. The appearance of the Biseks on the <u>British television</u> also had a negative character.

These were the reasons for the proposal to enter the Subject and his wife in the <u>Index of Undesirable Persons on 2/9/1985</u>. The proposal to include the named persons in the SSEP (*System of Unified Register of Findings*) was made at the same time.

Other contacts of the Subject with CIS (*Centre of Ideological Sabotage*) (besides aforementioned LOCHMAN, KARASEK, SOUKUP) include Jiri <u>BEDNAR, living in Great Britain</u> at present. It is known that BISEK has been friendly with BEDNAR since 1979. BISEK was a co-organiser of protests at the trial with the members of the CDUPP (*Committee for the Defence of Unjustly Persecuted Persons*) in 1979, where one of the sentenced was also Otka BEDNAROVA. A close friend of BISEK, Pavel HLAVAC, and his wife were also active there. It was found out in 1984 that Jiri BEDNAR informed his mother Otka that he directly recommended that BISEK emigrate to Great Britain, where he would be given a job and money. Then BEDNAROVA personally discussed everything with BISEK. After BISEK's arrival in Great Britain (July 1985) <u>BEDNAR really made all the arrangements for BISEK including customs inspection, accommodation and transport of their belongings to the current place of their residence in Cumbernauld</u>, Otka BEDNAROVA stayed in touch by writing letters to BISEK even when he was in Scotland.

It was found out in 1986 that BISEK wrote letters to CSSR. It is obvious from operative checks of these letters that the named is not very happy in his new situation. He complains about the heavy work load, his and his wife's and most of all their children's difficulties with the language. He is not satisfied with his financial situation either. This was supported by intelligence and through forced meetings with Pavel HLAVAC. All BISEK's children spent their summer holidays in CSSR in July 1986. They stayed with friends and relatives – the HLAVACS, DUSS, PIVONKAS, etc. PIVONKA and HLAVAC write letters to BISEK and inform him about the Church and the political situation in the CSSR. Letters were also exchanged between BEDNAROVA and BISEK in 1986. Lists of names:

<u>1/ BISEK's contacts in Great Britain</u>

HULBERT Alastair DOB 10.2.1941, 32 Dundas St. Edinburgh
OWEN Davis England
EUSTACE John – DOB 9.8.1949, Great Britain
HUNTER Andrew – DOB 26.1.1941, Great Britain
ROUSSEL John – DOB 11.2.1944, Great Britain, 2 Stocton Rd. Chorlton, Manchester
BROOKE Robert – DOB 12.11.1944, Great Britain
LLOYD Sally – DOB 17.2.1947, Great Britain

TURNER Gerald – DOB 8.9.1947, Great Britain
BEDNAR Jiri – DOB 3.7.1948, Great Britain
MORTON Andrew – DOB 24.5.1928, 121 George Street, Edinburgh, employee of the Church of Scotland
BURDEN Stan – 7 Barlow Road, Chichester, England
BROWNE (Family) – 9 Ballyhenry Drive, Newtonabbey, CO Antrim, Northern Ireland
COPE Mary – 100 Emscote Road, Warwick, Great Britain
BRAILSFORD E.N. – 6 High View, Portishead, Great Britain
NOBLE Adrian and Louise – The Lower Towers, Masson Rd., Batlock, Bath, England
PERKINS T.C. – 53 Broad View, Selsey, W. Sussex, England
BRASHER – Flat 14, Warner House, 2 Carverly Close, Beckenham, Kent, Great Britain
WILLIS J.F. – 78 Oxford Rd., Liverpool, England
LARKINS Peter and Elisabeth – 1 Mulberry Cath, Thorp Arch, Wetherby, Yorkshire, England
HODSON V.L. – 33 Rosemary Court, High Wycombe, Bucks, Great Britain
MCGHEE T. and S. – 23 Leven Ter., Carfin, Motherwell, Scotland
BISSET (Family) – 47 Airbles Cresc. Motherwell, Scotland
ROBAGLIATI D. and M. – 4 Wool Road, London, Great Britain
SWARBRICK Theresa – 18 Moss Lane, Garstang, Preston, Great Britain
HARLEY R. N. Holy Saviour Vicarage, 96 Lodge Road, Croydon, Great Britain
BURT Arthur – Peny Bryn Fram, Fforddy, Blaeman, Treuddyn, Mold, Wales
MUNRO Irene – Daliburgh Manse, South Uist, Scotland
LETCHER Cliff and Sue – St. Andrew's Church, Civic Square, Lauceston, Great Britain

2/ BISEK's main contacts in the CSSR

MAFERRAU Mario – DOB 23.11.1926, Italy, fy La Fiocondo sales rep.
RUBENSTEIN John – DOB 4.9.1051, USA
PEDERSEN Kirsten – DOB 26.4.1950, Denmark
LINDT Ruth – Germany
REED Barbara – New York, USA

LINDT Christine – Switzerland
KATSONIS Andrew – USA
GILBERT Harriet – DOB 22.1.1950, USA
WIDMANN Frank – DOB 28.4.1940, Germany
LOCHMAN Jan Milic – DOB 3.4.1922, Emigrant, Switzerland
KARASEK Svatopluk – DOB 18.10.1942, Emigrant, Switzerland
KOSLOWSKY Gerhard – DOB 8.11.1931, Germany
SOUKUP Karel – DOB 22.1.1951
KESSLER Hans – Switzerland
PUGH E.N. – USA
VAVRA Charles – DOB 15.1.1955
NIEUKERKEN Cato – DOB 24.6.1918, The Netherlands
KNIESTEDT Carla – DOB 6.5.1936
BOER Gysbert – DOB 10.7.1945
ERICKSON Florence – USA
WILSDORF Till – DOB 5.4.1940, Germany
PLECHATY Ivana – Switzerland
KAUDERS W. – USA
BREZINA Ales – DOB 12.7.1948, Emigrant, Canada

Due to the above mentioned facts, i.e. BISEK has emigrated and, at the same time, is no longer a citizen of the CSSR and is barred from entering the CSSR, it has been proposed to archive the personal file SAMOTA No. 9739 for the period of 15 years. All documentation, correspondence and other documents should be shredded. We will continue to watch him and follow his activities in connection with files SS RUZE (*Initial File Rose*) No, 11729 and SS VYSOCINA (*Initial File Uplands*) No 12847.

First Sergeant SYROVATKA Stan.

Superintendent Department 2 Capt. TUCEK Karel

Superintendent II Division of State Security Lt.Col. HAVRANEK Stan.

Appendix 2

WORLD MISSION LETTERS

THE CHURCH OF SCOTLAND

BOARD OF WORLD MISSION AND UNITY

At Edinburgh March 20, 1985

Which day the Board of World Mission and Unity being met and constituted.

<u>*Inter alia*</u>

85/18 **Evangelical Church of Czech Brethren.** - Reported that in the course of his visit to the Evangelical Church of Czech Brethren, the Rev. A. R. Morton had received a formal request from the Evangelical Church that the Church of Scotland receive into its service the Rev. Tomas Bisek, one of its ministers, who was highly regarded, who had studied in the United States and was proficient in English, and whose state permission to serve the church in Czechoslovakia had been withheld; and that the Department of Ministry and Mission had extended to him an offer of appointment as associate minister at Cumbernauld, Condorrat.

Agreed to be responsible for the arrangement and associated costs of initial settlement in Scotland of the Rev. Tomas Bisek, his wife and children, and to be fully associated with the invitation to him to enter the service of the Church.

Rev. T. W. Kiltie
Deputy General Secretary

THE CHURCH OF SCOTLAND

Department of
WORLD MISSION AND UNITY

121 GEORGE STREET,
EDINBURGH. EH2 4YN.
Tel. 031-225 5722

General Secretary:
Rev. D.H.S. LYON, M.A., B.D., S.T.M.

Telex messages are accepted for World Mission
& Unity by 72465 CHACOM EDIN for WMU
Grams: EVANGEL

ARM/AB

Rev. Andrew R. Morton, M.A., B.D.
Executive Secretary

17th June 1985

Rev. Tomáš Bisek,
Teleçí 129,
569 94,
Czechoslovakia.

Dear Tomáš,

This is simply a brief note to tell you that the address to which your boxes should be sent is

82 Cairngorm Gardens,
Balloch,
Eastfield,
Cumbernauld.

It was good to hear your news of your impending arrival. I wonder if it is possible for you to give now an approximate date. I myself will be on holiday in the first two weeks of July, and want to make arrangements for someone to act for me if you arrive while I am away. The people in the congregation are ready to welcome you, but other friends here would like to rally round for your arrival.

With all good wishes,

Yours sincerely,

Secretary.

Appendix 3

HOME OFFICE LETTER

Our Ref: B 414622/2 (S)

3 APR 1986

_Thank you for your letter of 11 February about the Reverend Thomas Bisek and his family, who are currently living in the United Kingdom.

I have noted that Mr Bisek's children wish to return to Czechoslovakia for a summer holiday and this is of course a matter entirely for Mr Bisek and his wife to decide. I am sure they are in the best position to judge the wisdom of such a visit in view of the circumstances of their departure from Czechoslovakia. However, I can say that when the family arrived in the United Kingdom on 10 July the children were in possession of valid Czech passports and if those documents remain valid they are free to travel on them. As visa nationals, the children will need to obtain re-entry visas before they leave the United Kingdom. To obtain these they will first need to apply for an extension of their current leave to remain here so that they have adequate permission to stay here when they apply at their nearest Passport Office for the re-entry visa. In the circumstances, if the children do intend to visit Czechoslovakia this summer, I would suggest that they apply to us as soon as possible for an extension of their current leave to remain so that the necessary formalities can be completed well in advance of their travel date.

Appendix 4

GOVERNMENT MOTION

447 *REVEREND TOMAS BISEK AND CZECHOSLOVAK GOVERNMENT*

Mr Norman Hogg
Mrs Margaret Ewing
Mrs Ray Michie
Mr Eric S. Heffer
Mr Allan Stewart
Mr A. J. Beith

★ 60

Mr Brian Wilson	Clare Short	Mr Adam Ingram
Mr David Amess	Mr Terry Lewis	Mr John McFall
Mr Jerry Hayes	Mr Eric Martlew	Mr D. N. Campbell-Savours
Mr A. Beaumont-Dark	Mr Ted Leadbitter	Mr Jimmy Dunnachie
Maria Fyfe	Mr Harry Ewing	Mr Allen McKay
Mr Alex Salmond	Mr Thomas Graham	Dr Lewis Moonie
Mr Malcolm Bruce	Mr John Fraser	Mr Eddie Loyden
Mr Hugo Summerson	Mr Stan Crowther	Mr Giles Radice
Mr Menzies Campbell	Mr Michael Welsh	Mr Ivan Lawrence
Sir Marcus Fox	Mr John Maxton	Mr Lawrence Cunliffe
Mr Steve Norris	Mr Sam Galbraith	Mr Tom Clarke
Mr Bob McTaggart	Mr Simon Burns	Mr Kevin Barron
Mr David Hinchliffe	Mr George Robertson	Mr Robin Corbett
Mr David Clelland	Mrs Gwyneth Dunwoody	Mr Stuart Randall
Mr John Garrett	Dr Norman A. Godman	Mr Nigel Spearing
Mr John McAllion	Mr Richard Caborn	Mr Bob Dunn
Mr James Molyneaux	Mr George Foulkes	Mr Terry Davis
Mr Ron Brown	Mr David Marshall	Mr Robert Parry

That this House notes with the deepest concern the decision of the Czechoslovak government to refuse entry to Czechoslovakia of the Reverend Tomas Bisek, Minister of the Church of Scotland at Condorrat Parish in the Parliamentary constituency of Cumbernauld and Kilsyth, to attend his mother's funeral; and recognises that this represents the lack of progress made by the Czechoslovak government in human rights.